Self, History and Future

A work on the modality of history (2015)

Circles of Identity (CI) are our tool of survival and have momenta based on their innate necessities. Rather than dividing history into past, present and future and attempt narrative analyses it is the search for these momenta that gives us historical insights. CIs move forward propelled by the necessity for parts to form a whole. The process of encompassments and tangencies is dynamic and fluid and it is this unstable but directional conditions that form history. As time passes there will be fewer and fewer CIs. However, the all encompassing final CI can only be in vacuum and will confront us with our destiny.

T. Iwamoto

Vernon Series in Philosophy

VERNON PRESS

www.vernonpress.com

In the Americas:	*In the rest of the world*
Vernon Press	Vernon Press
1000 N West Street,	C/Sancti Espiritu 17,
Suite 1200, Wilmington,	Malaga, 29006
Delaware 19801	Spain
United States	

Vernon Series in Philosophy

Library of Congress Control Number: 2015948250

ISBN: 978-1-62273-137-4

··· I decided to renounce them all and go into my own idea for good

Fyodor Dostoyevsky

From *The Adolescent*

Table of Contents

Overview and Summary

Assumption

There is a minor and thus far unsuccessful school of thought called 'Wholisticism' (more widely known as 'Holism'). I adopt the less used spelling because 'Holism' as a thought system is a failure. That is, once you admit an unexplainable totality you are on a slippery slope of allowing an 'indescribable'. It is a defeat for philosophy to come to rest in the comforting arms of an 'indescribable' even after any elaborate arguments. Philosophers should rather die fighting than acknowledging a quasi-religious graveyard of thought. 'Holism' is akin to a religion. It may keep a philosophical mask by inventing theology, but nevertheless an 'indescribable' is an admission of intellectual defeat. Boole, Frege, latter Wittgenstein are said to have been sympathetic to this idea of an indescribable whole. The totality of interconnected organic parts brings with it its own philosophical problems; e.g. take a whole language, how are all those parts connected, other than usages? What is this totality, in itself and in its relation to mind? How can it be described? Is its user part of this organic totality? etc.tc.. Here problems are as problematic as ones faced by logicists, formalists and intuitionists. The idea of a contextual wholeness eventually comes to an unexplainable whole. I subscribe to a 'Wholisticism', but, instead of practically giving up like Wittgenstein, hold the 'whole' —whatever it may be— accountable to describe itself. I tried it on formal logic ('The Elementals'[1]), on history (this work) and will try on numbers (next work).

---

[1] See http://philpapers.org/rec/IWATE

Put bluntly; 'a whole is more than the sum of parts' or '(x) › x' in my symbolism. But then, so what!? To say x=x because of (x), is nothing but metaphysics unless (x) and x can be connected by means of intelligible logical or mathematical operations. In another word '›' needs an operable meaning. Only in this way '(x) › x' can be promoted to a 'science' from a religion and should be able to 'demonstrate' x in a manner someway connected to our existing paradigm of understanding of everyday x. The above three mathematicians/ philosophers of maths were a little too shy to acknowledge a full-fledged 'Wholisticism' because they could not meaningfully represent a 'whole' without which formal logic was indeed nothing but tautologies and paradoxes as found out by Russell and Gödel. Given a number, say '3', although it appears to have a solid, independent meaning, this meaning entirely depends upon the structure of the totality of numbers. Set-theoretical answers of various kinds are attempts to construct (x) from x and ended up as notational gimmicks because the fabrication of a notation does not really answer the nature of (x). The von Neumann constructive notation of { } still does not tell you what 0 is, and what all those subsequent numbers are. It already assumes the ontology of numbers and only notationally constructs the epistemology of numbers. The notation of a process towards ∞ only calls for the good-naturedness of mind to accept that the notational process coincides with mental process or the structure of 'numbers' as objects, which remains unexplained. I am here to demonstrate how this idea of 'whole' works out on history.

Objective

For history to have a meaning one needs to grasp it as a structure of the totality of events. We have the past, a collection/chain (of chains) of events to guide us towards an underlining formula of events. This I seek in the functions of 'self'. Once correctly paraphrased 'self' should bridge the past and the future, and only this way we can talk about the totality of events, past and future. That is, the formula should be able to forecast the future events. These functions of 'self' are sought in 'Circle of Identity (CI)'. Although I quote some Freudian ideas in order to illustrate, CI is a concept of modal logic and has a wider, more abstract and operable meaning. CI has a structure, and I extrapolate it as the laws of CI, which guide us to an understanding of our current states of history and lead us to future predictions.

'Self' is a moving event with momentum acquired from the past and therefore has a direction. In contrast to Freudian concept of id/ego/superego, which is, at best, interpreted to explain each and every human in terms of contours of colours the three ingredients created by degrees of dynamic mixtures as results of environments and individual capacities, CIs are vehicles those individuals choose to drive through terrains of history. More id-orientated individuals may prefer certain types of vehicles, while more superego-aware people may adopt different models. Some vehicles carry a very limited number of passengers only for a short distance, some carry a large load for a very long journey, but both are vehicles nonetheless and have certain characteristics. It is these characteristics that explain history and future. The Freudian concept explains characters of passengers and to some extent societies those individuals create, and idealizes the future to be more superego-dominated. The concept is inflexible and not operable enough to predict the future. A CI is a concept that possesses inner driving forces of tangencies and encompassments and follows a direction it creates by itself. It is a modal concept of which 'self' is a variable.

Modus Operandi

The main theme of this work is the unfolding of the concept of CI. The philosophically not unimportant concept of 'self' in this context is merely a variable and is deemed unnecessary to be considered. I have no needs to colour 'self' as Freudian, Jungian, Post-

structuralist, etc.. 'Self' participates in a CI for various reasons: biological needs, psychological motivations, social conventions, religious convictions, etc., etc.. However, from a modalistic point of
view reasons are best left to each relevant discipline. I am only
concerned with necessities of x to become part of a CI in order to
form a whole. x cannot meaningfully exist without a CI, and a CI is
empty without x as it is the vehicle of necessity for x to navigate
'life'. Thus, CI(x) is a wholistic and modalistic concept with dynamism of operative meaning, which creates the logical progressions
of CI. There are many CIs as well as many types of CIs, but the nature of empirical CIs is, once again, best left to relevant specialists
because a coloured x narrows down the scope of CIs and distorts
any subsequent progressions. What matters are modalistic aspects
of CI as a logical concept. These are extrapolated as types and laws
of CIs.

The operative meaning of the colourless CI(x) is its internal
structure, which is a wholistic necessity that a whole is more than
the sum of its parts. This creates 'power'-relationships among various CIs, in that starting with '(x) › x (i.e. self-identified x is stronger
than naked individual x)' the numerical effects of membership of a
CI, the various structures and types of CIs, etc. form logical progressions. Alongside these progressions are power structures and a
certain necessary direction towards more and more encompassed
CIs. These arguments are also supplemented with illustrations
within my limited knowledge. From all these I will conjecture a
possible future.

Achievement

From the application of wholistic concept and methodology on
history I identified tangencies and encompassments as moving
parts of CIs which create a direction of history as the end-point of
CI encompassments. This is accompanied with the establishment
of the laws of CI and various empirical consequences and observa-

tions, such as the vertical power structure of nationhood CIs, which are the most predominant current CI, is being flattened. There may or may not be actions and reactions, but this horizontalization is part of a logical process towards less and less CIs and is not a temporary phenomenon. Merging mind through internet and social networking, the rise of human rights, gender equality, etc. should be interpreted as necessary components of horizontalization and logical encompassments. I further predict this process will produce the emergence of more horizontal nationhood CIs with less money-orientated structure, eventually to end with a completely horizontal final intellectual CI, maybe assisted by more aggressive roles of artificial intelligence. There will also be unforeseen consequences alongside this process, because of the unpreparedness of political mindsets and systems for new phenomena, the emergence of new socio-economic models based on complete gender equality, which may give rise to i.e. the decline of consumption-focused economy, generally less creativity coming from the removal of gender-focused mindsets and merging mind, expectations for more professionalism in politics, etc.. These logical, analytical and narrative arguments are not only something of a novelty but hopefully will also act as a source of imagination.

From my text it will become clear that the dominance of our current nationhood CIs is by no means absolute or secure and that our current period should be viewed as a turning-point in history, to move from the hitherto accepted norm (be it proxy democracy, market economy or money-based vertical social structures) to a new paradigm of more horizontal, human rights-entrenched and eusocial structure with intertwined and interconnected common mindsets. This trend is not a one-off phenomenon. It is a logical process based on a wholistic necessity.

Contextualization
(Foucault & Fukuyama)

It was suggested by some reviewers and publishers that my work would benefit from being contextualized to similar contemporary works so that readers can position my ideas in relation to some other better known interpretations of similar ideas. This immediately reminded me of Foucault's idea of interrelated 'power-knowledge', which talks about a system of references where any 'discourses' inevitably get lodged so that they invariably end up part of 'knowledge' which is mired with 'power'. This sounds like a touch of 'Wholisticism' of power, which constructs 'current truth'. Although I see some conceptual dynamism in his 'power-knowledge', it is too skewed to an effort to interpret a modern society. Rather than going deeper in Foucault's thoughts I quote a joke in the shape of an existentialistic paradox of reference; according to Foucault a theory only has 'current truth' through a wholistic system of references. If so, Foucault's theory only has 'current truth', which means it can be true or it can be false, depending on 'power' *in situ*. Since Foucault is primarily a power-antagonist, Foucault is probably not in favour with 'power'. Thus, as part of 'power-knowledge' Foucault's theory is false. If so, his idea of 'power-knowledge' is false. No wonder Foucault is a pessimist, of which he is. This shows he is right about his pessimistic theory, which contradicts his pessimism. Therefore, he should be an optimist, of which he is not. A further complication arises in the shape of an editor who thinks it is a good idea to contextualize my work on 'logical truth' in Foucauldian system of references so that it will be part of 'discourses' to be understood better and inevitably gets tainted by 'power-knowledge,' where 'logical truth' becomes 'current truth.' If so, 'logical truth' can be true or false. Thus, my work does not have 'logical truth.' Then, the editor, by encouraging my work to be contextualized, destroys my work. Now this is against his intended purpose. Therefore, I should de-contextualize. But, in order to de-contextualize what is already contextualized I have further to contextualize in the context of de-contextualization. This puts more value to my work by being entangled with Foucault's good name, but reduces value by being foolish enough to confuse 'logical truth' with 'current truth.' etc.. This is typically an existentialistic view on the world, while the world remains the same whether viewed by existentialists or by logicists. Foucault may not be an existentialist, but he is deeply in grand continental tradition of thinking, where presumably because we are part of 'life' or because we are 'life', thinking everything in the context of 'life' is taken for granted, forgetting we are equally, and maybe separately, part of 'universe' and of 'everything.' One day I might be tempted to write a book about it

Foucault's 'discourse' is a muddled notion entrenched in the politics of nationhood and modern world. His 'language' as medium of 'power-knowledge' points to a 'Wholisticism' in the sense that it tries to work up some unity of everyday political reality and its directional creativity, albeit disdainfully to Foucault. His 'discourses' may 'network' us, but do not lead us to any 'whole' because power is not necessarily inclusively juxtaposed to our 'self.' I further argue that what gives 'discourses' its centripetal force is not their association with power but their political usages to conjure 'benefits.' Think of Hitler's speeches or Churchill's oratories in the name of nationhood. Powers of 'discourses' are not orientated in knowledge but in arbitrary promises of 'benefits' by disreputable political conjurers. Besides, Foucault's ideas are too preoccupied with the present and fail to point to any future other than that results from continuous struggles and resistances between 'power-knowledge' and us, 'cultivator of the self,' under such a domination. It may explain some aspect of empirical 'reality' today but ignore potential dynamism of mind, free from any political reality. My work is such an example. There is no metaphysical power absolute that gives 'discourses' a centripetal force. It is rhetorical emphasis on 'benefits' that brings power to a certain usage of language. Power has to metamorphose into everyday something tangible of its possessor (and its cronies), benefits of present and/or future values. It is here power absolute becomes power relative, something metaphysical degrades into something empirical. Foucault is a thinker half full as philosopher, half empty as political antagonist. He is tainted because he is personally and emotionally entrenched in power present and empirical and tries to extrapolate something more universal and permanent. If you try to work out 'power' from power, you have to exhaust all empirical powers, which Foucault does not appear to. On the other hand, to try to extrapolate power from 'power' you need a sound logical reasoning backed by good illustrations. I take the latter albeit far from being successful.

Likewise, Fukuyama's 'end of history' and 'last man' are both mechanistic notions in that a political ideology such as 'liberal democracy' pinnacles human desires and thoughts and fails to incorporate dynamic potential of mind. 'Liberal democracy' is just a name given to an aspect of a contemporary political system as seen in some developed Western nations. It may be currently predominant in some nations, but is neither universal nor permanent. It is desirable, no doubt. However, one cannot extrapolate the future of political history and propensity of human behaviours from such a simple notion. 'Liberal democracy' is too static a concept to capture its potential, and maybe subtle, transformations. As it is also a creation of mind it can metamorphose or mutate into any shapes and shades via surreptitious changes in laws, administrative by-laws and even tax rules, and still nominally levelled 'liberal democracy,' which, at its very extreme, is in the mind of beholders, like Democratic People's Republic of Korea. Things human, whether some "-isms" or institutions, are not set in stone. They can transcend into something noble when inspired by superhuman deeds (e.g. Mandela's ANC) or degenerate into some lowly codes of conducts (e.g. benefits grabbing corruption of ANC once in power). In wanting to glance into the future you need a more dynamic concept with operative meaning. All isms are human institutions based on 'desirables'; 'economic well-beings promoted through a tax system which favours individual talents and toils', 'social fairness on the principle of 'liberté, égalité, fraternité,'' 'equal distributions in order to prevent social divisions,' 'something for nothing,' 'more for less,' etc.. What is desirable varies depending on demand and supply, availability, demography, geopolitics, group psyche and psychology, etc.. It is the conceptual search for the modality of desirables that captures what to come to form our future. In contrast to Fukuyama's 'liberal democracy' I propose the idea of CI. 'CI' is a notion to describe history taken as a 'whole,' which does not distinguish the past and the future. Everything is in the present, which represents the past and the future as momenta. 'Liberal democracy' is a name given to a parametric constraint of a nationhood CI, and a nationhood CI is nothing but one stage of CI progressions. Given 'last man' without the final encompassing CI based on merged mind and accumulated stock of knowledge, it will be a fecund potato field to produce criminals and addicts. In fact that is how history started, i.e. the conquest of weaklings for the pleasure of the ancestors of today's royals. So Fukuyama's 'last man' is rather the beginning of history. Anyway, before his 'last man' trundles along, it is more likely we will see the dominance of artificial intelligence (AI). AI already governs from our ballistic defence system and air traffic control to power-transmission and banking. It is more fruitful to contemplate our future with post-singularity AI (AI with a 'self') than worrying about our man losing his libido to strive.

Be it Foucault's insight into a society based on 'power-knowledge' or Fukuyama's attempts to predict the future based on the end-game situation of 'liberal democracy,' both are like trying to work out a curvature of a line from a given point by using pre-calculus maths. No amount of elaborate narratives based on a quasi-dynamic, phenomenological concept like 'discourses' or a static concept like 'liberal democracy' will capture the dynamism of moving events and their fluid directions called 'future.' You need the methodology of operative concepts that process moving events.

I attached this maybe controversial and deliberately confrontational paragraph so that readers might see how a difference in approaches to similar subject-matters produces mutually divergent conclusions and insights. I acknowledge I am not a scholar of either thinker and have not even seriously read them as well as being nil-influenced. In case there are readers more familiar with the quoted thinkers, I apologize if there should be any misquotes. Any quotations are only there to serve to illustrate my conceptual and methodological differences.

Finally

This work was conceived and written from autumn 2014 to spring 2015 in 6 months, and all the 8 chapters were written simultaneously. It was pointed out from publishers that the structure of text does not seem to follow the natural thought process and that the lack of references makes it difficult to evaluate. However, whatever I wrote was primarily thought of by myself, and I hardly owe anything to anyone without being intellectually pompous. I have little interest in any contemporary philosophers and I do not seriously read but some classical works on philosophy of logic. Events and terms quoted and used in this work are mostly embedded in our language as common knowledge, like some Freudian terms. Quotes and references are not really central to my core theme of CI and its logical progressions, they (even misquotes if there should be) are only there for illustrations. Anyway, in our age of Google readers can so easily verify them via on-line searches.

Chapter Résumé

The below is a concise résumé of each chapter, and I coded its relevance to the main theme of CI evolution (*** very ** moderately * distantly).

Chapter 1 (*)

The general background to my ideas. The epistemological value of history as knowledge is very limited due to inherent difficulties of reconstructing past events, and because so much depends on interpretational skills and luck of hitting good materials. I thus advocate an intellectual approach based on considerations on the modality of history.

Chapter 2 (**)

I introduce the concept of the circles of identity (CI) as the foundation of my philosophy of history.

Chapter 3 (***)

The detailed expansions of the idea of CI as a logical and modalistic concept together with narrative illustrations of the historical developments of CIs as I empirically observe.

I highlight nationhood CIs as most pre-eminent in our recent history and predict its inevitable transformations into something more flattened.

Chapter 4 (***)

From a wholistic hypothesis I extrapolate basic laws of CIs, with logical progressions towards the final CI. Theoretical arguments are furnished with many illustrations so that readers will not get bored.

Chapter 5 (***)

While the laws of CI predict the encompassments as the natural evolution of CIs, to result in an over all encompassing CI, which is in vacuum, the process is itself dynamic caused by types of members and of CIs as well as relations among CIs. Once again arguments are furnished with many illustrations.

Chapter 6 (**)

This is an attempt to schematize chapters 3, 4 and 5 into a conceptually compact, notationally streamlined format. However, because modal logic is not really axiomatic as formal logic, this is really an attempt for theoretical summery.

Chapter 7 (**)

I take most important and thematic agendas of today and consider them one by one from an angle with emphasis on the concept of CI.

Chapter 8 (***)

I predict and speculate our future as an extension of logical developments of CI. Along the path towards the end-point of CI progressions our vertically orientated social structures will be replaced by more and more horizontal ones. At some point, artificial intelligence is likely to trigger singularity (this is one of topics in my next work) and impact our future, contributing towards horizontalization anyway.

From the above it follows that the shortest way to read this work would be 3→4→5→8, if you are more generous with your patience, 3→4→5→6→7→8. Only if you are most kind, then you might care to read them all.

January 2016, Author

1. Preface

In contrast to my other work 'The Elementals' this is an essay and more a work of art rather than a work of philosophy or logic despite the usage of the word 'logic.' Although I could go to a great length to emphasize my point of view by constructing an example of elaborate arguments, I would rather hope to leave that task to someone else (someone with more profound background knowledge in history) and simply concentrate on showing a direction by introducing some new concepts as guiding principles of history.

In historical descriptions it is generally agreed that time passes 1-dimensionally, in which events occur causally and maybe progressively, individuals have freewill and are conscious and proactive players in those events. Thus history is deemed to be formed by men of action and fame; we come to achieve an understanding of our past via chronological descriptions of those men, who influenced, and were influenced by, other men in relation to various significant events that concerned them and bear causal influences on us today. The course of history is generally seen to be a linear progression with circular elements being straightened by the steady accumulation of scientific knowledge. However, are we intelligent enough to keep advancing the frontier and depth of our knowledge ever and ever? Without ever-advancing stock of knowledge history may become circular, rather than linear progression. I question here how really we are intelligent enough to make us believe in our history and destiny.

Any readings of the future depend on quasi-analytical disciplines such as economics, politics, sociology, psychology, anthropology, archaeology, etc. as well as spontaneity allowed by freewill and ingenuity originated in intellectual mind not necessarily subject to causality. The future therefore contains something not always predictable even if given all information available today.

Study of history is only useful in as much as it gives some guide-lines to current participants as to likely effects of similar events, but it cannot predicts any outcomes, although optimists prevail so long as we can keep increasing our stock of knowledge.

In contrast there are attempts to understand history by means of ideas, be it Hegelian dialectical principles, Marxist materialism, Mill's utilitarianism, Malthusian catastrophe, Freudian theory of personality or supra-personal concepts like staatsräson, autopoiesis, categorical imperative, autonomy, prudential restraint, etc.. However, events as outcomes of human behaviours have too many variables to be coherently formulated into satisfactory explanatory theories. They may shed light on some aspect of history, but any claim to a definitive understanding ends up as a self-defeating shortcoming. Not everything in history is socio-economic phenomena as much as history is not really reducible into psychology or ethics.

Empiricism *a la* Ranke, although it on surface appears less fanciful than idealistic intellectual history, faces as many difficulties as any court case. Narrative history can be as ingenious as criminals trying to escape justice. After all, most things said and done by public figures are highly manipulative and inventive, and historians' works become as subjective as their interpretational skills. From an audience's point of view no doubt some are on the mark, but some are not, also depending upon audience's ability to judge historians. This is very much as skilful art work as sleuth games and not satisfactorily trustworthy especially as future guidance. Ranke, the father of modern empirical history, is already giving way to philosophical history, in that Burckhardt could not help conceptualizing history as an inevitable function of culture, religion and state. Meinecke saw everything in statehood.

Further I am not inclined to agree that geniuses play very significant roles in history, not that they are insignificant in their contributions, but that their periodic appearances are already incorporated in the making of history. Men like Newton, Darwin and Einstein would have appeared more or less at designated times, considering the states of impetus in thinking at the time, which borrowed a faculty of a genius to express itself in a most revealing and crystallised way. That is, geniuses are idiosyncratic in the sense they leapfrog the abilities of many clever but ordinary minds, but not totally spontaneous in the sense they too owe their ideas to a larger current carried on the shoulders of those mortals. One only has to remind oneself that calculus was discovered/invented almost simultaneously but independently hundreds of miles apart (there was even a slightly earlier Japanese contemporary who came close to a similar level to Newton/Leibniz independently and via less refined notation), or that Darwinism had a philosophical counterpart, Organicism by Schelling, not far apart in time. Needless to say, even greatest men in politics like Napoleon or Marx,etc. are hardly a genius, but rather men of time and place. Geniuses are probabilistically destined to appear in our history as idiosyncratic but nevertheless vehicles of linearmomentum of human intelligence.

My essay here is not an attempt to present a pseudo-analytical theory of history by presenting an over-simplified formula to complex problems. It is rather a question to see if we are not creating a problem for ourselves for vainglorious representation of ourselves, i.e. are we not fooling ourselves by thinking that we are a special species at the top of biological tree and are uniquely placed in a position to judge all things small and large from human perspectives. Are we really so unique as to deserve a record of ourselves as a knowledge on par with scientific knowledge? The history of mankind other than the accumulated total of scientific (or more preferably objective) knowledge is the story of squabbles, squanders and gossips. At best it is more a work of art based on pretensions, interpretations and imaginations, and thus lacks objective basis to be knowledge.

Think about the days of kings and nobles in position of influence, which seemed to have dominated much of our history until recently. It is not much more than the history of greed, intrigues, power and manipulations to satisfy their thinly veiled Freudian ego. What can one derive from any studies of descriptions of such events other than entertainment values? Today kings and nobles are replaced by celebrities fashioned in the name of democracy but in reality chosen by the media, which may or may not have biased views and which are, if anything, mediocre or worse in intellectual capacity. It is not even actual persons who are chosen, but rather their images carefully spinned and disinformed by them and their PR that are voted for. Their actions are also constrained by the necessity of their image making, so they feel compelled to act in ways consistent with their own images.

Events are not any nobler or less personal than centuries ago. Behaviours of states are often as juvenile as delinquent school children. One cannot even be bothered to enumerate up-to-date examples. Only have a look at any newspapers at hand. Didn't we recently have some spectacularly scandalous buffoon as a many-time elected prime minister of a major European country, and another who allegedly lied to start a war to appease a misguided world power? This US connection even appears to have served well personally for his post PM careers. These are just two of many so-called leaders of the world, whose smooth talking mediocrity attracted mass sympathy to start a career which did not end well, except monetarily. Needless to say there are many more examples of even less savoury nature.

There is little to tell between camouflaged self-interest and public interest since no one is going to confess their own baseness. Democratic processes mean little when promises are made and broken easily. Without much to account for, politicians and voters are aligned mostly for short-term interest regardless of long-term costs to future generations, not only for ourselves but also for all life forms. Economic models are skewed towards consumptions, profits and immediate financial rewards, which are products of some biased and over-simplified theories of human behaviour dating back to the age of the Industrial Revolution, at which time one did not fully realize the scale of human greed and stupidity, and one did not have to worry much about waste and the environment.

Inherently faulty and weak democratic processes, systemic un-accountability, disproportionate influences of the media exacerbated by the advent of IT, celebrity culture combined with more and more human rights without due obligations at a time population is increasing completely out of step with the availability of natural resources, these call for new political systems and economic models developed and adjusted through trials and errors. We have a new apparatus worth trying at least, which allows us a direct democratic participation and which is already making a serious inroad into our economy.

The weakness of parliamentary democracy should be implemented by direct power of removing those in public office by way of an internet referendum when serious misconduct surfaces, possibly administered by an independently elected internet administrator. The result is, any powers exercised in the name of false democracy will be curtailed and thus empowered people will be able to experiment with bolder candidates without fear of entrusting too much on someone not really known. Given proper checks and balances what we need is something akin to a well-chosen benevolent dictator - not politicians who say what voters want to hear and cannot make decisions, other than those which please voters but are accompanied by dire financial consequences as witnessed recently. We are at a political and economic junction to try to find an alternative model for the future, although in reality we are likely to carry on until some catastrophe forces us to change.

Likewise, the economy should be reconstructed not based on how to consume and waste but based on how to endure and save. This can be done by encouraging companies to produce goods that are efficient and sturdy. Political willpower should be there to introduce a tax system that prices in waste and environmental costs. Public education should be in place to condemn fashion for the sake of consumption. We have the means of achieving all this save for the sadly degenerate current political system which centres on cheap populism and short-termism in fear of electoral cycles.

However, I am here not to ponder rhetoric away from today's reality. I am not interested to affect people to change for the better. I leave that to high minded politicians if there should be any or to inevitable catastrophes long overdue. What will follow, will follow. I am here to predict what awaits us by current momentum. I suppose I am proposing an idea to understand and predict history. Hopefully not many people will read this, so the possibility of this idea interacting with a course of history is reliably small. Further I intend to propagate intellectualism for distant future generations to survive the remnants of the faulty democracy and egoism that seems to rule our foreseeable history.

I do not foresee limitless progresses based on scientific knowledge like H. G. Wells. No matter what knowledge we may attain we, as part of nature, are still ultimately confined within necessities of nature. Scientific knowledge will confirm this rather than help us to transcend the laws of nature. Knowledge in this sense will provide us with the comfort of knowing our limits and forces us to exercise prudential restraints to maximize our resources. Scientific knowledge is vanguard of our defence against our egoism as individuals. We as species supersede us as individuals much as a circle of identity is not a voluntary umbrella for individuals to pick and choose but something inherent in us all to be of ourselves.

I would like to advocate a Burckhardtian 'culture' to seek and widen our circle of identity. This will lead us to our inevitable destiny, come what may. Meaningful democracy can only be achieved by better educated public and their realizing the widest possible circle of identity. The study of history of culture is ultimately the study of the development of our circle of identity. If we can find the rules of circles of identity, this will lead us to find the momentum where the past and present is taking us to. As Burckhardt saw the 'psyche' of era and nation through the insight into art and culture, I try to capture the 'psyche' of our existence through the insight into our circle of identity. This is the cultural study of our circles of identity.

2. Philosophy of History

To break life into '*erat, est and fuit*' drives us to Zeno-like paradoxes. To juxtapose history with the future is itself a contradiction, especially if you believe in freewill. History can only be about past events, and the future is a nonentity by definition, like trying to capture death as if it is a mathematical limit of life. Even past events are not self-evident in the sense that they are always results of interpretations, scientific or otherwise. See any court cases how difficult it is to reconstruct even a most immediate event by using scientific tools and live witnesses, let alone events in the distant past. No matter how many documentary evidences are given, there will be no historical event that can be safely established in a court of law.

Furthermore, history is tainted by so-called winners and ones with loud voice, while losers, silent and decent ones who prefer *sotto voce* or cannot even be bothered to speak out are conveniently ignored, in the similar way a personal history is rich with good and trifle memories worth remembering but often leaves out unpleasant, and maybe very important, ones out of consciousness, hence creating jobs for psychoanalysts. Thus, history may give distorted and maybe unfairly rosy pictures, which affect our perception of the future. Unsafely reconstructed events combined with conveniently chosen topicality makes history an unsavoury way of apprehending ourselves and therefore our ability to forecast the future. The loud and rich history of e.g. Christianity and western civilization contrasts well with the largely silent e.g. African history, where human communities existed much longer than anywhere else. However, it is dogmatic to think that therefore we have much more to learn from the former. Maybe there are many hidden lessons and interesting episodes in the latter, which could be uncannily useful in canvassing the future.

What constitutes history and the future is a moving self with momentum acquired through necessities. Necessities are first and foremost biological as without a physical body we cannot exist. As with 'The Grapes of Wrath' we do not have to go back centuries to find out how basics can affect our life given slightly changed circumstances even in the richest country today. A few climatic catastrophes will bring about serious politico-economical changes despite diversified risks because of wide-spread trade relationships as already apparent with less developed economies. Other necessities are supplementary but psychologically as demanding once biological necessities are fulfilled, which is not difficult in the age of relative plenty, human rights and social benefits.

These necessities relate to security and satisfaction. The consciousness of self is necessarily forward-looking as self is only aware of life and the present. For a self there are no past or future, it is always the awareness of the present. The past and future are already part of the moving present, so to speak. The satisfaction of the present must contain the security of the future. To this end the current self tries to ensure as much predictability of the future as possible. For example, our heavily monetized economy manifests this necessity as propensity to secure and save as much monetary assets as possible, even if it grossly exceeds the likely needs for the future. Likewise, other psychological needs such as power, fame, personal attractiveness, etc.. also relate to the security of the future with some oscillation due to differing personality profiles. So-called riches are men over-ridden with miscalculated propensity. In other words, they are as stupid as those who cannot adequately provide for themselves.

The reconstruction of the past and the future from the moving present depends upon finding the circles of identity (CI). A circle of identity is the way a self leverages itself in order to be most economic with its purpose of biological survival and control. An individual naturally extends to a family, which expands into a kinship group. This is so because, first of all, there will be no biological survival for a single individual, and because a group is stronger than an individual in terms of efficiency of shared workloads and insurance of mutual dependency. A community is also more efficient than a mere collection of solitary individuals and families for the sake of biological survival. Therefore, an individual consciously or unconsciously seeks a circle of identity as extension of its existence.

CIs of many levels and nature constitute history. As will be extrapolated later, CIs have rules of function in that they seek tangencies and encompassments in order to enhance benefits, without which membership is doomed in the longer term. In addition to these natural tendencies, events are today so intertwined via the internet and social media that history is no longer a chronological causal collection of sporadic independent events. It is becoming an organic continuous event span across national borders and with a time scale where the chaos theory (maybe due to our merging mind with denser and faster connections between people, of expectations, imaginations and interpretations) is more applicable than ever. The world of multi-speeds is also converging into a single speed. I do not know about the butterfly in South America, but a man burnt to death in Tunisia did cause a chain of events, which was initially received with enthusiasm in the West but turned distinctly sour as people in the West did not quite realize what democracy meant in the Arab world. The Arab Spring quickly mutated into the sand storm and it was a presentiment of ill-fortunes lasting to this day. One can metaphorically say that a street vendor in Tunisia dealt a death blow to a notorious dictator in Libya without lifting a finger, did serious damages to a few more dictators and their cronies and, in the process, even administered a *coup de grâce* to the already tarnished reputation of a certain former British prime minister. After-effects still smoulder at forefronts of many Middle Eastern nations. All this could not have happened without the new media and shows humanity and nations are getting entangled. We have never been better informed of day to day events across the world and furthermore can communicate with each other instantaneously, spontaneously and cost-free. No wonder CIA is keen to monitor. For them this much information flow must be like a honey pot dangling in front of the nose of a bear.

The evolution of CIs is steadily moving toward the all encompassing CI, which will have a hitherto unforeseen consequence for benefits creation. That is, historically benefits are created ostensibly or surreptitiously at the expense of other CIs and non-members. The emergence of the all encompassing CI will make it necessary to produce tangible benefits without any exclusions and dilutions of benefits to other CIs and non-members as there will be none as such. This is a situation never seen in history and tests the human ability to its limits. The all encompassing CI with universal membership has little tangible membership benefits to distribute. There should be no inner CIs to benefit at the expense of peripheral members and non-members. Nevertheless, this CI will require a structure in order to govern itself. In the long run, tangible benefits are the most efficient means of mobilizing and motivating humans. Benefits without socio-economic elements will require satisfactions beyond psychological and fictional pleasures. I will term this new type of benefits intellectual benefits. For this to be viable, our so-called 'democracy' has to be transformed from the democracy of instant gratification and short-term benefits to the democracy of well-educated, from the democracy of individuals to the democracy of spices, from the democracy of humans to the democracy of all things small and large on earth, maybe beyond.

However, before we reach the all encompassing CI there will be many transitory phases, the process of which will be also helped by catastrophes of one kind or another. Catastrophes work as catalyst for changes for our mindsets and various institutional creations, which are to some degree historical coincidences and to which we adhere because we as a mass are not capable of any drastic changes willingly. We always prefer devils we know than any unknown abysses. This is also consistent with the nature of CIs because groups, especially of democratic tendencies, tend to be skewed towards average mentality, if not the lowest common denominator (one hopes not). Otherwise, this process towards the final CI may take much longer as the end product of slow eliminations and, meanwhile, events may not wait for us to sit and watch the world go by, like I am doing. The precarious positions we are in, are due to our uncontrolled appetite to breed and 'enjoy' ourselves at the expense of future generations and other species. So much condensed population with so much energy devoted for our individual comforts and petty desires, make the time scale of any disasters much shrunk and more devastating.

Catastrophes are plenty in making both as man-made and genuinely natural, including cosmic ones; in history we observe many of both. They clear a new way for thinking and provide a new room for rebuilding. It is our business to prepare so that both thinking and rebuilding will be of benefits to the process towards a more encompassing CI. If so-called historians wish to be useful, one of the best things they can do is to show that human creativity was observed better at times of social chaos and provided for new foundations for culture and institutions. Just think of Renaissance or inventions at the time of World War (WW) I and II. It is not a coincidence that one observes disproportional creativity at times of social disruptions, like before, between-times and aftermath of great wars because this is when one is relatively freed from the social cliché and stereotypes, and from the mental and physical bounds of the *status quo*, and maybe because one realizes one only has a limited time even to be creative.

Many great novels saw prolific flowerings such as by the likes of Dostoevsky and Walter Scott to pay-off impending debts, gambling debts at that in case of the former. It was towards the end of tsarist Russia, at a time of social unrests and tensions that one found greatest ever literally talents. It was not in the affluent comfort of ordered Victorian middle class that Dickens found his great stories, but in the pits of anarchic East End poverty, so unbefitting to the wealth of the greatest ever empire. Renaissance was at a time of wars and chaos and produced our treasures of best artistic talents. All our current contemporary life owes more or less to the inventions and discoveries relating to the two great world wars. We owe so much not to peaceful tranquillity and comfort but to unrest and insecurity.

Historically speaking, we live in an age of unprecedented peace and material riches, although it sounds contradictory and the prevalence of media makes it sound prevaricated. That is, the intensive and instant news flows of daily deaths by terrorism, small wars and epidemics here and there and hideous crimes from all four corners of the world, give us the opposite impression. These were previously either unreported through the lack of available media or deemed not news worthy among too many similar or worse incidents. It is only a recent phenomenon that, say, any unusual death of an individual hundreds of miles away should become news and a dozen unusual survivors of some disaster become world celebrities.

The entwinement of societies and communities via the new media is a precursor to an encompassment of CIs. This is all the more reason to think we are paradoxically and surreptitiously waiting an unthinkable catastrophe while enjoying a rare moment of quiet and peace, combined with unprecedented resilience owing to mutual insurance based on socio-economic interdependence. However, we are not in control of ourselves, let alone of nature. Given all those incentives, talents and tools of analyses, we could not even control our economies. We do our best to outsmart each other and find loopholes in laws, IT systems/trading algorithms and business models rather than work in tandem towards a solution except when survivals are at stake.

We are aware of problems facing our societies but yet unable to break through nationhood CIs. Most of our daily life is ruled by nationhood CIs and accompanying bureaucracies. We take it for granted that nationhood CIs are the supreme adjudicators of everything we do. However, a nationhood CI is itself our invention of not long ago, which, with dysfunctional parliamentary democracy and social/cultural dead ends that appear to confront us, needs reinvention. Given the tight holds nationhood CIs exercise on us, it is with catastrophes that we will leap forward towards a higher encompassment.

Meinecke saw a divinity in nationhood CIs. This divinity had its days in WW I and II. Yet, we expected the conscience of victors will redeem nationhood CIs and demonstrate that if not nationalism, then democracy prevailed on mankind, possibly allowing noble-mindedness to take us into hidden depths of our mind and culture. Democracy did prevail, but it only seems to remind us we are hopelessly petty and superficial. When politics becomes family businesses and celebrities are voted in lieu of genuine leaders, 'democracy' is a byword for the failure of modus operandi. The idea may be right, but the 19th century method of choosing is according a platform to the 21st century imagery based on 20th century propaganda. The result is we are being led by people who lead by being led by their imagery. So the thrice diluted images of ourselves are engaged to tackle our undiluted problems. No wonder we are not getting anywhere.

We henceforth await cathartic catastrophes, without which the encompassment process takes much longer and which force us to face our self-made dead ends and take us to rigorous tangencies to confront impeding nationhood CIs. Many of our present values are intricately and inherently connected and intertwined with nationhood CIs, be they cultures, religions, politics, economies, literatures, music, paintings, sciences and engineering, etc., as they developed together with nationhood CIs over the last three centuries, even though most of them pre-existed nationhood CIs.

The feeling of dead-end is also the feeling of the end of nationhood CIs in terms of their contributions towards our creativity. We feel we can no longer create by means of, and in support of, nationhood CIs as nationhood CIs lose their distinctiveness, as we are aware nationhood CIs are going rather than coming. In this twilight age of nationhood CIs we, however, are not yet sure what will come next. Nationhood CIs are still too powerful for us to imagine the next stage and even to dream of the possible world CI. Meanwhile, many phenomena are subtly and obviously challenging the demarcation of nationhood CIs at every level of our sense of values from personal to old-fashioned national politics. This is the source of our feelings of dead-end. Yet, we are too impatient to wait for the encompassment process to take place naturally. Thus, my longing for catastrophes as catalyst. Besides, like run of the mill economic forecasts our mindsets are too skewed towards linear projections, which often go wrong as economists should know.

The most outstanding features of this dead-end feelings are the lack of initiative to establish the new authority that should gradually replace nationhood CIs. Despite globalization, cross-border networking, internet entwinements, etc.., —call them as you wish—, it is the still powerful nationhood CI bureaucracies that dominate our daily life as it is in the self-interest of nationhood CIs not to give way to anything that might weaken their grip. This subtle but powerful conflict is probably the biggest obstacle to our next stage. Since this next stage is intentionally as well as unconsciously unplanned, it only appears as unfathomed abyss rather than unscaled heights to political planners, observers and bystanders. However, my own feeling is that our new democracy will be administered by the new media, i.e. the voted internet administrators supported by voted policies-making boards, in conjunction with artificial intelligence. Current incumbents may put any numbers of obstacles and excuses, but there is no way the next phase of democracy, if indeed it is that, cannot embrace this new media. This will probably be one of the biggest game-changers for centuries.

Through the new media in not too distant future our mindsets will converge as a prelude to, or as a part of, a more encompassing CI. It would, then, be feasible to replace physical wars with games, provided that it can be established thatgames and wars have a consistent relationship. In our times, wars bring no benefits economically whoever wins or loses. At last, we will able to emulate some animals which are wise enough to engage in mock fights instead of real life or death battles. The unprofitable consequences of war even for the victor were first noticed at the Russo-Japanese war, one of the first modern wars with long-range naval battles envisaging dreadnought developments as well as barbed wires and machineguns where the process of war devastatingly dragged on against the anticipation of either, and were confirmed at WW I and

II. The advent of drones is the first step toward the game-like wars and here we will see a new breed of physically unfit and mentally warped heroes, a predecessor of which are probably financial traders and algorithmic trading systems. This, in fact, is already the case with strategic wars and tactical nuclear wars, where game-like simulations are literally proxy wars. That is exactly why we never had to see nuclear wars. As wars go, terroristic guerrilla wars is little more than nuisance and only termed 'war' by way of political exaggeration. In the logic of CIs terrorists can never form any encompassing CIs.

The decline of nationhood CIs will be augmented by the social media which function as voting navigator and promote intelligent voting. This are a higher style of voting and goes for one's preferred form of governance rather than one's natural choice. This only became possible with the advent of social media which can legitimately play useful real-time roles to canvass and intelligently guide participants to vote not to endow any particular party with overwhelming power . This is useful as democracy becomes a dysfunctional tail-chasing dog. Then it might at least turn into a direct consensual democracy instead of a failed proxy democracy.

3. Circle of Identity (CI)

A circle of identity (CI) is an association an individual (member) imposes upon himself in order to benefit from his affiliation with an organization. This can happen unconsciously as, for instance, with a family group, or consciously as with a political institution. It can also develop naturally or semiconsciously like religious influence on children via family involvements. An association is generally a social structure centred on anything that promote a bond among members, but can consist of only one member in some cases. Benefits derived are often ultimately socio-economical, but can be psychological or even fictional. They range from the imaginary benefits of psychopaths to the concrete material benefits of baksheesh, from the defensive benefits of not being ostracized to the benefits of active manipulators. CIs may be sustained for a short time on psychological bases. However, they will not survive long without tangible benefits.

It should be acknowledged that 'benefits' is a murky concept that allows a great deal of subjectivity. It could even be antisocial or criminal, allowing for psychological diversity. However, in order for CIs to grow and become substantial, it has to be largely socio-economic and mostly monetarily translatable because benefits are derived from human relations and are used to cultivate human welfares.

Furthermore, a CI has a serious drawback in that whatever is directly associated with it tends to be wholeheartedly justified in it, no matter how wasteful and ridiculous it is on reflection. One typical example would be a war and a nationhood CI. What is most important for CI membership is their own welfare, and CIs are basically and essentially a vehicle for the achievement of their welfare. Nationhood CIs are no exceptions, they came into existence and are sustained for their benefits, which surely include membership welfares. Wars are most wasteful consumptions and meaningless destructions (of humans and natural resources) for all parties concerned. They benefit nobody. They occur because of human mismanagement at the top. Nevertheless, they glorify and even honour those responsible and those who were sacrificed in the name of a nationhood CI. If only you view a CI just as a CI (a human convention) and as nothing terribly special unlike Meinecke I have to emphasize, then you will find how ridiculous it is to get involved in any wars and even more so to find any glory in them. It is in the name of a nationhood CI that one forgets a CI exists for us, and not the other way around. However, even this drawback has its own function, in that it provides CIs with dynamisms, i.e. tangencies and encompassments to move forward and eventually to weed out those CIs which fail to deliver net benefits in historical contexts. In a CI we become blind to faults of that CI, and it is probably necessary to move that CI to its end, i.e. to encompass or to be encompassed. This applies to any CIs. Likewise, in corporate CIs we often do unethical things in the name of a 'job'. Examples are innumerable.

The simplest CI is that of a self-identity, that is, of being conscious of oneself set against the so-called world. A 'self' here is a variable 'x' that satisfies a number of CIs (can be one) in various relations to each other ('inclusion' being the most prominent one) and is uniquely identified as an individual 'a' in a limited context. That is, 'x' sees itself through a CI and become a 'self'. Being aware of oneself as member, or even as non-member, of any social group, is the state of a CI. This contrasts with simple individuals. Non-CI individuals are like Freudian id, while ego is already a state of CI. Super-ego is the rules of CI. There is an element of symbiotic communality in the development of CIs. From individuals arise isolated communities as there are more benefits for individuals via organizations. Various conflicts among organizations are suppressed for the sake of more efficient organizations because more efficient organizations afford more benefits and eventually more members. In the process, stronger and stronger common identities, e.g. linguistic communalities, cultures and institutional religions, etc., produce multiple layered and more and more encompassing CIs, which in turn go through similar processes to arrive at even more encompassing CIs. An encompassing CI contains subjugating CIs as well as mitochondrial enclosures like mythological adoption of conquered gods. The former is simply overlapped by the encompassing CI like a Christian culture and a church; the latter represents interactions between a CI and an encompassing CI in a way that is beneficial for both by overcoming elements of conflict. This requires intelligent accommodation of an encompassing CI by the mitochondrial CI, but not vice versa. A mitochondrial CI is characterised by its thin wall in order to maximize benefits by proactively mingling with the larger host CI. In contrast to this, a parasitic CI has a thick wall to try to secure benefits via explicit exclusion of non-members, which is generally counter-productive as exclusion tend to work two ways and make it more difficult to interact with the host CI.

The widest circle of identity is the entire universe. However, since we do not really know what the universe is like, this would not normally apply and realistically we have to settle for the entire life forms on earth for the time being. The smallest circle of identity is the Freudian ego (self-identified id) so that we satisfy our biological self in a socially measured manner, which is more effective and beneficial in the end. In between, we have a large number of animate and inanimate circles of identity, which stands on an equal ground in terms of their captive ability but ordered by personal preference. The reason why one chooses a certain circle over another is not important as this is not a psychology essay. For intellectual, cultural, religious or/and any accidental reasons one decides to adopt a number of circles with a certain order and become a member, which constitute various groups, which in turn form a tangible society. It is thus that e.g. 'dog and his master' sadly do not form a CI for the lack of the capacity of tangencies and encompassments, for not having human sophistications such as the faculties of betrayal, double-crossing and pretence.

A society has a momentum which is in large part based on commonest ground among commonest circles. Thus, if the Freudian ego is the commonest circle and the necessity to feed oneself is the commonest ground, then the ease and difficulty of obtaining food are the momentum for one to adopt a certain circle, and the more of us choose this circle, the more dominant this circle become and benefits members. This is so because the more of us belong to a certain circle, this circle is more influential over other circles with fewer members and makes it easy to achieve its primary target. This is how we decide to belong to a certain group, be it religious, military or political, etc. Being its member brings about the ego related benefits at various levels depending upon his ability to adapt in the circle by applying intelligence, physical attractions, biological connections, etc. Therefore, the Freudian ego is the smallest but also the core circle in the sense that it is beneficial to hide its true scale in order to be more effective in achieving its primary purpose, whatever that may be.

In general a CI does not exist in a vacuum because generally no benefits can be derived from a vacuum. Without benefits to bestow a CI will be memberless, except where benefits are imaginary. The only exception is a CI with only one member where benefits are imaginary but nonetheless real. However, with nothing to react with, even this type of CI will struggle to survive. Where there is more than one member, this type of CI gets feebler as member numbers increase because with multiple members a CI becomes a social institution and has to seek socio-economic interactions in order to supplement imaginary benefits with socially acceptable benefits.

This is often the case with religious CIs. So-called 'spiritual' benefits may give rise to bonding effects. However, once a religious CI becomes a social institution, without socio-economic benefits, it cannot maintain its institutional footings and fails its members. The founding fathers of a religious IC are therefore people who laid out practical mechanisms of institutional survival. The socio-economic transformation of a religious CI usually leads to religiously contentless social convention, where a religion is a thinly veiled bonding principle and members derive benefits via socio-economic mutual favours at the exclusion of non-members. The like of the Freemasonry epitomizes this type of CIs. The desire to purge elements of socio-economic benefits from a CI often leads to its own institutional denial. It is the failure to grasp the distinction between a church as a socio-economic institution and one as a spiritual institution that created many martyrs like Girolamo Savonarola. Once you realize they are separate entities, it is not contradictory to see so many immoral behaviours in a church (or any religious organizations). It's naming as such reflects confusion: the only pure religious CI is a one-man CI content with imaginary benefits. No wonder churches keep reinventing themselves to suit the current of time e.g. by inventing 'miracles' or rewriting theologies.

Insofar as a CI cannot exist in the vacuum, a CI has an optimal number of members. This is so because it is the nature of socio-economic interactions unique to that institution that determines an ideal number of memberships. The stronger the bonding principles and the bigger the derivable benefits are, the larger an institution can be. As religions lose their grip, generally religious institutions become weaker. A degree of so-called 'religiously motivated' violence is no measure for the strength of a religious institution. As it becomes apparent that violence ultimately bears no benefits, no religious institutions will prosper. It does not even require the trend of a secularity to see the decline of religious entities. Diminished benefits and the strength of an encompassing CI will bring about the ever declining religious elements of a CI. The less an optimal number of members is, the weaker a CI becomes, as it interacts less with other socio-economic CIs. Therefore, it is a fate of every CI to try to increase its membership. The only way to succeed is to create genuine benefits; any violence-generated PR will eventually exacerbate its own demise.

If a CI can only exist among other CIs so that they interact in order to create benefits, then CIs have a structure such that 1) they are encompassed by a higher and higher CI, and 2) this process itself has a structure whereby a CI is either wholly encompassed, partially encompassed, or excluded, by another. This process will dynamically lead to the widest and most embracing CI, which is in the vacuum and therefore, in order not to collapse unto itself, it

requires its own negative CI to counterbalance, i.e. to be surrounded by the despair and fear of its own extinction. Ultimately,
our goal is tautologically to survive for the sake of survival. We exist
in order to exist. For this end, we will be governed by scientific
needs and all our resources should be directed for the optimal efficiency to balance our finality. It is only when this all embracing CI
is achieved that we will be rationally pursuing to secure our survival in the most physical sense of the word.

That is, all our socio-economic activities will be directed at increasing our objective knowledge in order to ensure our survival in
a most cost-efficient way. At the end of non-circular, i.e. linear,
trajectory of history individuals exist for the species and the species exists for its identity and survival. Survival can only be attained via knowledge. This is the pragmatic aim of science and is
called intellectualism. Assuming no supernatural, and psychology
removed, CIs are destined to become more and more contentless
except for their initial formations, while their benefits must remain
real. CIs with various colours and sizes will lose their individuali-
ties as they move toward a higher and higher CI. This is so because
the more encompassing a CI is, the less exclusive its character has
to be. This can only be done by the accumulation of objective
knowledge, which eliminates overlaps and exclusions via better
communal understanding through our humanity.

A wider and more embracing CI complies with the laws of CI.
The fading of religious, gender, racial, nationalistic colours, etc., is
compatible with this requirement for the widening of CI. While a
lower CI tends to have a down to earth character, and thus although it creates a stronger bond, it is also in conflict with many
surrounding CIs. For a higher CI to embrace lower CIs without de-
ploying conflicts, it can only do so with knowledge and education.
As socio-economic benefits are eventually derived from other CIs,
that is, as it is the nature of any purchasing power to oblige some
CI to serve some other CI, at the top of tree a CI will fail to deliver
any benefits. Without any socio-economic interactions, the character of the all-embracing CI has to be most accommodating in the
sense that its denial destroys all its benefits. This contrasts with a

lower CI, which provides specific benefits to its members and does not hesitate over conflicts, physical or otherwise, if necessary.

This encompassing CI is compatible with the concept of the merging mind. Reflect on our desires for 'proofs' (most typically in maths and logic), 'debates,' 'discussions,' 'persuasions', in fact any forms of communications, these point to merging mind and eventually merged mind as a matter of CI progressions. So far we had tall walls, 'cultural,' 'linguistic,' 'geographical,' 'ideological,'etc.., etc.. We now have for the first time in history a practical means of dismantling these walls gradually but steadily in the form of intertwined and interrelated minds through internet. This will in turn further accelerate CI progressions, along with less and less creativity and more and more artificial intelligence. Merging mind is self-fulfilling function of mind towards the wholeness of mind, where 'proofs' are no longer required. In this process females will play a bigger role through their more social or eusocial nature. This intertwined and more feminine eusocial environment is an inevitable destiny of CI, which I may not necessarily like, but luckily it will not come in my days. Here mind is ready to coexist with (or more likely, to be enslaved by) artificial intelligence (PSAI). The asset side of this balance sheet is fewer conflicts and stresses. Managed stability. What a comforting thought for our doting days.

Coming down to earth and applying this view to the current political scenery, it is EU, not UK, which is on the right track. EU is now encountering one of many hurdles it has to go through to reach a supra-nationhood statue. Any downsizing of a nationhood CI is a political failure, while the current attempt of creating a new region-based CI is an effort worth praising. Likewise, the seeming flexibility of a religious CI as observed via the accommodation of e.g. various gender issues or theological transformations is compatible with the necessities for a higher CI.

It should be noted that severe mental illnesses profess lack of self-identity or confused identities. People with such problems are often encouraged to express themselves so that well-layered identities can be found around a self-identity. Through expressing oneself one contextualises oneself in one's self-interest as well as in one's relationship to others. It accentuates and clarifies one's position in a wider context and helps one to form most beneficial relationships materially and mentally. It is not only people who are susceptible to mental illnesses. Institutions are just as fallible, as CIs can be individuals or institutions, which are basically groups of people.

Mental illnesses vary from

$(x \rightarrow (y \mid z))$ to $(\Psi \wedge \sim\Psi)$

It is the necessity of finding a whole out of parts that causes a mental illness. Thus, neither $y \mid z$ nor $\Psi \wedge \sim\Psi$ per se is an illness. They are rather states of affairs that are endowed with innate dynamisms that transform them through tangencies and encompassments. Therefore,

$y \mid z$ could be $(y(z))$ or $(z(y))$, and

$\Psi \wedge \sim\Psi$ could be $\Psi \rightarrow \sim\Psi$.

Schematically representing a CI as a circle, a circle can only be drawn from a point in the centre, which is a conscious self. Where there is no identifiable self, there is no CI. Any state of madness hampers the formation of viable CIs. Thus, a circle (CI) always assumes a point (conscious self) inside. When an idea (identifying object) takes over the self, i.e. a CI without the centre, this is a state of schizophrenia. This contrasts with a simple self-identified CI, which is a one-man religion. Likewise, when an idea takes over a complex CI, this creates an institutional schizophrenia.

The easiest extension of a simple self-identified CI is a biological CI as members are readily identifiable via blood-relations. This can easily further extend by including distant biological relations and quasi-biological relations and give rise to a primitive tribe. A medieval power mechanism based on courtly apparatus is basically the extension of a tribal structure strengthened by matrimonies and furnished with titles and feudal privileges and duties. A paradigm shift caused by the misbalance of benefits and exclusion opened a direction toward nationhood CIs as society progressed from an agricultural economy to an industrial economy. Napoleon and Bismarck were the early witnesses to this trend. Many quasi-religious and paramilitary orders saw their decline as the relative weight of benefits derivable dwindled in accordance with the exponential growth and diversification of socio-economic activities alongside industrialization, not because of scientific proliferation.

A CI is generally recognized as against other CIs and does not exist in vacuum, so to speak. This is so because what bind a CI are benefits of membership, which are not available to non-members. A benefit is consciously or unconsciously an advantage leveraged through the organizational strength which is set against other organizations. When it appears to exist on its own, i.e. in vacuum, it is deriving imaginary strength through membership of fictional organization, whereby the strength is real in terms of mental endurability. For example someone engaged in some personal mysticism who believes in being favoured by this mystical entity may show remarkable strength of mind as much as a misguided politician who happened to be favoured by fortune of time. This strength is his ability to believe in himself regardless of socio-economic reality. It can have a moment of its own.

Thus a CI can be political, cultural, religious, economical, biological or even imaginary; indeed anything that promotes a group structure. The most potential CI is an association with a lynchpin social or pseudo-social idea where members are conscious and therefore active, where benefits are socio-economical at the expense of non-members, the best examples would be the likes of the Nazi party, the soviet style communist party or today's Chinese communist party. The least influential one would be a one member association centred on a mystical idea, e.g. one man religion, which seeks no other members, where benefits are psychological. In between the most common CIs are corporate CIs. Every CI at every stage utilizes various tools of bonding such as ideologies and theologies of various kinds, fictional or real common enemies, honours, favours, music, songs, totems, budges, ceremonies, uniforms, etc., etc.

I would like to emphasize that it is an organization through a CI that is more important than an ideology behind a CI. Thus, take for example communism. A communist CI may initiate, cement and promote an organization but is eventually superseded by the organization itself. It may be a cause of an organization, but not a *raison d'être* for it. It is for this reason that e.g. an ideology may become obsolete, but an organization may still prosper as long as membership brings about benefits. One only need to remember that in the post-cold war Eastern Europe it was often ex-party members who prospered though membership bond, or in today's China a party membership is more important than any ideological belief, if any. Likewise, in religion an idea may have found an organization, but it is the organization that creates a theology and even outlives a theology, like many of today's religions. This is why theologies evolve in accordance with the needs of the times.

It is noteworthy that imperialism and religions in the form of religious missions went hand in hand to create a more convenient and subservient colonial CI, be it Spaniards, Portuguese or British. This shows how adaptive religions are as institutions.

It should be noted that CIs can go dormant and get resuscitated. Bonds that give rise to CIs can be invigorated by benefits formation. If benefits are pumped in for whatever reasons, e.g. for a political purpose, CIs will be rejuvenated and become functional. Depending upon how natural and strong bonds are, CIs have potential uses for manipulators who are prepared to fund benefits.

Thus, CIs themselves hardly have hard cores. They consist in social bonds supported by socio-economic benefits. Take the cold war confrontation, where two politico-economical CIs appear to have excluded each other. However, communism and capitalism only happened to fashion those CIs with superficial bonding principles and by themselves they are neither right nor wrong. It is a function of benefits that allowed one to encompass the other through tangency. Making observations on religious CIs, they were quick to adapt themselves once the sea of changes swept them from political arena with the emergence of nationhood CIs. They were often encompassed by nationhood CIs as part of bonding principles, where ceremonies were as important as theologies, and flexibility was the key feature of their survival tools.

Every CI at every stage utilizes various tools of bonding as mentioned above. This can be most evidently seen in military organizations. They are fossils of our primitive mentality manifested through CIs. CIs expend great costs and energy for bonding as well as providing benefits. In struggles with other CIs for tangible benefits at their expense it is the strength of bonding that is the most deciding factor. A member or CI that reflects the prevalent moods and characters of the encompassing CI becomes the leading opinion maker of that CI, be it a top-down or bottom-up. However, a good leader is one who leads while being led. A vile leader is one who pretends to be led in order to lead. The problem of spin-led democracy is the difficulty to distinguish the two, as the two are occasionally transmutable. This is where the ingenuity of man can temporally rule over the logic of CI, which, however, inevitably regains its wits as long as men are imposed with waning life.

CI can be broadly classified into a top-down CI or a bottom-up CI, where the latter can be regarded as more resilient or stronger, but of course the organizational momentum sometimes plays a role in obscuring the difference. Membership can be active or passive, and often changes according to levels of benefits. Therefore one can say that a bottom-up CI with more active members has the most potential to prevail, while a top-down CI tends to have less but more dominant active members, which can be strength as well as weakness. A cult religious or fanatical politico-military group is a good example. Leonidas' Sparta is at the zenith of the top-down CI, while Napoleon's France at its glory shows that a top-down CI had its moment in almost merging with a bottom-up CI. However, although they may enjoy a temporal strength, this tends not to last very long as the top layer is often too confined, dogmatic and volatile. Furthermore, passive members tend to join a top-down CI not because of proactively seeking benefits but rather from the fear of losing out on benefits. A top-down CI is inherently less stable as the thin top layer manipulates the large passive members. It is akin to a fighter jet in which instability creates manoeuvrability. Counter-intuitive, but structurally it is more complex and could lead to institutional mental illness. This is often the case with a CI with militaristic tendency, and its weakness is infrastructural endurability which needs the constant support of passive members. Therefore a top-down CI can literally topple over, while a bottom-up CI tends to fade away as it goes out of fashion, so to speak.

Today the most widespread CI is a nationhood CI, but it is historically a quite recent phenomenon. The most successful introduction is by Napoleon who inspired fellow Frenchmen with patriotism cum socio-economic benefits derived from military successes as can be glimpsed in '*Le Rouge et le Noir*'. It is his new 'national' army fortified with industrial scale artillery and the French nationhood CI that temporally ruled Europe in early 19th century. Just as we see the success of an exemplary top-down CI in Napoleon, one also simultaneously observes its fatal weakness in Napoleon's sudden change of fortunes. Ironically a nationhood CI is, according to '*La Marseillaise*', akin to a ship. A nationhood CI developed in Europe following the French Revolution as an obvious replacement to waning power structures based on religions and aristocratic landownership.

It should be noted that some nationhood CIs were forced or heavily influenced by empire-builders. Germany (Bismarck), Italy (Garibaldi),

Japan (Meiji Restoration) are thus late-comers of nationhood CIs. Some were consciously created (many nations in Africa, Middle East and, of course, India and Pakistan/Bangladesh) for the convenience of empires. Take the example of Japan. Until mid-19th century most ordinary Japanese never heard of an emperor, and the nation consisted of almost 60 autonomous feudal clans (more accurately about 300, but many were affiliates of larger parent clans), whose lords were literally the centre of universe for citizens of each clan. Thus, the collapse of those little feudal nationhood CIs in 1868 suddenly spewed out talents to be utilized by the new centralized nationhood CI and provided it with engines for growth. Prior to that citizens were confined within each clan, and each clan had to make do with whatever talents available within its border. Now, the new central government had not only a new CI under the figurehead of newly discovered ancient institution of emperor but also an inexhaustible supply of unemployed but educated, cheap and mobile talents to be picked and utilized, with their utmost gratitude. With the guiding examples of empire built by leading nations of the day, Japan had an impetus to move forward to become one of them, rather than one of the many conquered. Probably much the same can be said about Germany and Italy.

This is a typical example of the dynamics of CIs with less numbers and more power concentration moving forward. Taking the above example it was the tangency of US in competition with Asian ambitions of major European empires like British and French to move across the Pacific that awakened Japan in 1853 with ocean-going frigates supplemented with steam engine and equipped with cannons to fire explosive shells with superior accuracy and range. Japan by then had the knowledge of the Opium War and the fate of weakling nations as witnessed in Shanghai by some farsighted observers including some leading figures of the revolution (most famously Takasugi). This led to the deliberate change of the regime from the feudal system based on agricultural cum mercantile economy to the more modern top-down centralized, industrial trading nation with well-equipped army and navy. Despite of the sudden nature (i.e. the Shogunate regime was still very powerful in 1853), it took a mere 15 years for the complete overhaul of regime change with the various unimplementable false pretexts of the reinstallation of the ancient imperial system and the expulsion of foreign powers as there was no time to educate and enlighten those who were blind to impending crises of imperialistic invasions pending slightest excuses. Counting nationhood CIs alone the number shrank from more than 60 to 1 in 15 years. Many so-called revolutionaries kept the change of heart in disguise for the sake of the national unity and achieving the regime change and only afterward implemented it as the exact reversal of the previous official policies of 'back to the old' and 'anti-foreigners'. These 15 years were probably one of the most exciting periods not only in Japanese history, but also in the history of the world, and show a power game at its most extreme and intricate with interplays of realities and pretences, conflux of cultures, histories and religions and decisive balances between fast evolving arms and politico-military powers. Out of 100 nations in a similar scenario only 1 or 2 will come out as successfully. This extraordinary escape from the clutches of imperialism came about because the two sides of the potentially fatal civil war surreptitiously understood each other under the yet unfathomed new nationhood CI despite the still strong clan-based mindsets each and every player belonged to.

Japan was thus set free from the Shogunate power apparatus to the state machinery geared to military expansion and economic growth based on industrialization assisted by the numerical law of CIs. Once given this impetus, the long tradition of crafts including those of learning, the national, slightly paranoiac psyche for curiosity, attention to details and social cohesion helped that country to more than catch up with the western powers, culminating in the complete defeat of Russia in the Russo-Japanese war of 1904-1905. This was also the beginning of the process of the fall of the Tsarist Russia. This psyche owes its origin to the tightly knit agricultural society confined in geographical isolation and once again came to rescue after WW II, which this time brought the paradigm law of CIs. That is, the shift of its CI from top-down to bottom-up liberated highly versatile talents from the less flexible class system and invigorated the CI with new energies for growth.

In the aftermath of civil unrest any new CI would naturally be top-down and in the hands of those who took leadership in the struggle. This took its course as it does with the inner parasitic circle, i.e. the externalization of internal problems, paradigmatic limitations embedded in political thinking and the exhaustion of human resources confined within the inner circle, and led to yet another phase of unrest leading to WW II. What took place after that is a paradigm shift from the top-down to the bottom-up with a result of more talent and resources released from the class system making use of new opportunities and create growth, not unlike release of energy at the shift of the feudal clan system to the modern centralized system. It was many non-Zaibatsu new enterprises that brought prosperity to post WW II class-free Japan.

This post-WW II recovery was no doubt easier compared with what took place after the 1853-1868 period because it involved less of a mindset transformation. Having availed itself with the two laws of CIs Japan now faces a new challenge. With the CI status quo unchanged Japan needs a new impetus in the face of declining population, the loss of momentum from WW II recovery and political stalemates (i.e. consensus-driven politicians not known for any leadership qualities doubly weakened by the loss of direction in the maze of globalization).

If I venture to answer in the spirit of this work it will come from the 'horizontalization' of a CI. A CI has a vertical power structure necessary for tangencies and encompassments. However, as CIs progress there will be less and less CIs and more power concentration, which eventually should result in the final CI in vacuum, which, with no more CIs to encompass, should have a horizontal structure. Although Japan is nowhere near to this final CI, it is uniquely isolated geographically, culturally and linguistically, and in addition in terms of mindset, which is uniquely innocent from the lack of friction with outside elements. What I see is a pseudo-horizontalization of its CI in the face of the brick wall it now faces. Not a willing solution, but nevertheless probably the only way out by default. Foremost part of the 'horizontalization' is radical gender equalization. As it derived energies for growth from the numerical effects of CIs and the revitalization from the paradigm shift of a CI, now it should attempt to reenergize itself from the 'horizontalization' of a CI via gender equalization, which is a combination of the numerical effects ($2 \to 1$) as well as paradigm shift ($\forall \to H$).

With the drip-feeding of gender equalization the problem of population decline will be addressed as population here means workers. Moreover, akin to the numerical effects and the paradigm shift, this horizontalization should release talents and human recourses necessary to energize the waning CI ('akin' because of the unknown factor of power structure to accommodate 'horizontalization'). Women in Japan hitherto took less active roles compared to the western counterparts, whether from tradition or female wisdom (mens' stress for power is womens' longer and better life, especially now as they enjoy fair protection under the law) I do not know. Nevertheless, there is more room left for them to move up and fill in, be it government posts, corporate boards or every run of the mill job, including the police and the military. Japan is relatively uniquely positioned to take advantage of this possibility because of the culture of strong social cohesion and education, while in many other countries aggressive gender equalization, if possible at all, will have a considerable negative side at least to start with.

The wholehearted embrace of female empowerment is Japan's third arrow of CI evolution, by default this time. This is not just rhetoric enshrined in the law but a complete sea change of social attitudes, i.e. a mindset revolution as happened twice before. Gender equalization, together with the other factors already mentioned, may act as a catalyst for horizontalization and may contribute to a new CI as an unintended consequence. Although nationhood CIs are doomed, once horizontalized they will together move up to a new encompassing CI. What may come after is probably the global horizontalization assisted by the new media, the collapse of party political systems and the eusocial female liaison enhanced by its empowerment. This is not to do with whether males like or allow it, but a part of the laws of CI. The horizontalized nationhood CIs will together form a grouping and bring about benefits to each other. Becoming essential part of this process is the only way out for the flagging Japanese nationhood CI.

I have dwelled on a single example for too long, so now let us turn our to other examples and resume a brief anthology of nationhood and other CIs. It is in the process of a nationhood CI that e.g. the Russian serf emancipation took place. Following the Napoleonic and Crimean wars it became more obvious that social cohesion was necessary to establish a stronger nationhood CI. Its implementation delay was due to the precarious decision making of a

weak top down CI in the latter days of Tsarist Russia, a fatal structural flaw which resulted in the revolutionary movements.

Let me cite some examples. For instance, the USSR nationhood
CI is regarded top-down because it contained the inner manipulative CI (the communist party), which encouraged their doctrine to
justify their existence and promoted membership in return for
benefits, which incidentally in the process of disintegration spitted
out an innermost CI consisting of security forces like KGB and part
of GRU. This core CI metamorphosed itself into mafia-style organizations supported by nothing but active members whose reason
d'être is solely to benefit themselves at any costs at the expense of
any non-related entities, thus revealing the ego-centred nature of a
primitive CI. We see many remnants of this former core group in
the top echelon of today's Russian political and economical circles.

A top-down nationhood CI tends towards nationalism and this
works so long as there is enough space to distribute benefits due to
growth. When this stalls it will be forced to find more artificial
means, such as external threats, ideas, etc.. This is so that members of the inner CI can keep enjoying benefits at the expense of
peripheral members when the dialectic contradiction becomes
obvious and the dual system fails. The active members of the inner
CI then turn into the self-interested mafia group in order to maintain their status-quo benefits totally regardless of any disadvantages of anyone else (members or otherwise).

Likewise, a similar course might be found in China's today and
tomorrow. Its strength on surface is likely to be surprisingly brittle
once this manipulation loses its grip through the loss of economic
momentum as the drip-feedings of growth bonus peters out and
fails to reach more and more populace, while the core CI tries to
retain less available benefits to themselves. This should call for
caution on the linear projection of optimism about China (already
happening). The often-mentioned unique strength of Chinese civilization, which lends a myth to the pseudo-sovereign cultural supremacy, is itself a myth as China cannot remain a cultural island
surrounded by what they colloquially regarded as barbarians like

the Mongols or Manchurians or foreign devils like Americans or Europeans, without losing affinity benefits with the democratic free world. The cultural ingestion of foreign devils is no longer feasible as China itself is drowned in the sea of information and integrated into more and more homogeneous culture of the world, or in short Americanised. Today's Li Bai (a renowned 6th century Chinese poet), if not a country party official, would be sophisticated enough to accept minor corruption, most likely drives a BMW, gets drunk on good malt whisky while twittering on an Apple iPhone, may even go to MacDonald's. It should be remembered that when one talks about Chinese civilization, it is in the context of China's drowning foreign invaders in its culture, not the other way around. China never culturally drowned even its nearest neighbours like Japan, Korea or even Tibet or Mongolia. So when one talks about Chinese supremacy it only means the sheer volume of population facing any invaders. That, however, without the top-down approach, could easily mean disintegration under its own weight. Its size is strength as well as weakness, and does not automatically lead to the guaranteed notion of economic hegemony. The bottom-up China is yet to see its day even after some 3,000 years. Its policy of population control is, although less stringent today, in the self-interest of top-down political style, as well-off population means better-educated populace which contraindicates a controlling inner CI. That is, by its sheer size of population the wealth per capita is self-imposed with limitations within the controllability of a top-down CI.

China's nationalistic CI strengthened by new moneyed mass populace choreographed under the banner of the communist party has no encompassing power unless it incorporates more interactive elements. This could for example happen through a more inclusive culture and *bona fide* international cooperation. As the Chinese have done in their long history, they should explore new dimensions of some hitherto unimagined innovative culture to contribute to the riches of the world and earn international respect.

Extending examples to other corners of the world, problems of Middle East and Africa largely stem from the lack of natural borders, reflecting the colonial past of most of the countries concerned. This means a weak or sometimes even non-existent nationhood CI is often exploited by a more natural CI like a tribe or religious sect. That is, a strong but smaller CI within a weak nationhood CI functions as a manipulative inner IC for its benefits at the expense of the rest of the country. Despite many names given to the problems of the region, the volatility and instability that characterises it is pretty much the historical fault of Western exploitation. They will need a transition to more naturally drawn CIs to rebalance the region. The Pandora's Box that unleashed terrorism can only be closed after more violence to redraw natural borders to accommodate more stable CIs.

Interference with the natural process of formation of a CI, for whatever reasons, generally only complicates the process not only for the interfered but also for the interferer, without any desired effects. This is because a tangency inserted by the interferer has two ways and can backfire, and because the interference is often initiated by sentiment rather than by necessity, without full commitment. This situation will be exacerbated especially if CIs are mutually exclusive. Roman interference with Early Christianity and the recent Iraq situation are good examples.

Similarly an empire is a deformed top-down quasi-nationhood CI where a nation plays an inner manipulative CI at the expense of peripheral CIs. Benefits are skewed towards the inner CI and the empire stays only so long as it has a growth momentum which allows temporary discrepancy of unequal benefits because growth makes the measurements of benefits relative and dynamic. It is when growth peters out that an empire realizes it is not really a united CI, but a group of repressed CIs under manipulation of the inner CI.

WW I and II mark the end of old-fashioned geographical empires and moved our history onto the dual empires of Soviet style top-down ideology in the name of socialistic equity and bottom-up money democracy under the guise of market economy, where the static former could not fund enough benefits to hold together nationhood CIs and the cyclically dynamic latter only produced such uneven benefits as to render its superficially open society horizontally and vertically undemocratic. Thus, stripped of various illusions, we are once again faced with naked nationhood CIs which are being driven to the wall with struggles not only with each other, but also over economic growth based on greed and consumptions and social cohesion wrapped under human rights of diversity in religions, cultures, sexualities, ethnicities, etc., etc.

Individuals who supported nationhood CIs —sometimes even unconditionally— are now empowered to confront those same CIs. In the reverse manner of speech from some assassinated US president, it is nationhood CIs that exist for the welfare of individuals, because while individuals are real, CIs are our inventions. 'Human rights' is the byword that signals this reversal. If there is an enforcement process that institutionalizes and consolidates human rights, that will be the beginning of the end for nationhood CIs. This is probably where the borderless new social media come in. They will generally work to weaken nationhood CIs as they legitimately question the validity of proxy democracy which has so often disappointed them.

Nationhood CIs, which, in order to hold together, produced empires, market economies, various ideologies of governance and ownership, etc.., are now under attack from individuals who demand freedom from the legacies of nationhood CIs in the name of human rights. Here, individuals are no longer citizens who are happy to sacrifice for the sake of a nation, but rather independent mindsets who, by birth right, expect less interference from a nation.

I view so-called terrorism as a form of institutional schizophrenia owing to conflicting and confusing CIs. The ultimate rationale and salvation of a terroristic CI lies in creative destruction which restore some order to benefit members rather than sacrifice members. Religious fanaticism is only a borrowed front for appearance to arm relatively uneducated and naïve recruits. It is not helpful to seek causes of terrorism in theologies. Let's hope in the rubbles of seemingly senseless terrorist violence lie compromises and solutions for stability. The creation of a new CI that brings basic material benefits is the only way out. This is a CI based on something to lose rather than nothing to lose; egocentric self-preservation rather than *schadenfreude*-an self-sacrifice. Anyway, in an environment where the death of a soldier becomes a national headline, there is little chance of defeating the regime where the death of a thousand is no news or rather a celebration of heroism. The alternative is to become as ruthless and aggressive as the opponents, but soldiers of so-called civilized nations are more like fighting civil servants looking for pensions, not the brutalized warriors they should be. The worst enemy of a civilized army is its own media and so-called human rights lawyers looking for business, rather than Kalashnikov carrying illiterate peasants. If we are too civilized to call for a level fighting ground adjusted to the lowest common denominator, then we are already a lost cause for a war. There is nothing civilized in any acts of war, political correctness is a luxury misconceived by politicians who lost street wisdom and is purchased by the blood of anyone except their own.

Touching so-called more developed countries, the US enjoys a super nationhood status as historical accidents favoured the establishment of a federal structure over multiple individual states each large enough as to merit nationhood. Weak CIs at the level of individual states make a stronger nationhood CI possible, which is leveraged by mitochondrial CIs like the Jewish CI and active multinational academic communities that give, take, and tend to invigorate the nationhood CI. As to the hegemonial ambitions of the likes of China and Russia, I would not be overtly concerned as they are simply incapable of exerting any useful international influence or control in so far as they remain top-down, and needless to say the US has sufficient military capacity to counter any opportunistic military adventurism. The bottom-up US and the world at large will never be taken over by any top-down nationhood CI because their dual structure is incompatible with the plainer structure of the bottom-up nationhood CI, in the sense the core CI can only retain its status quo in its established manipulative relationship with the passive members. In trying to establish the treble structure the core CI enters the uncharted territory under the new dynamics of power structure. This is why any large scale military conquests of more democratic forces of considerable size do not generally have a sustaining power as can be seen in the Mongol conquest of China or the USSR's adventures on various satellite nations.

It is noteworthy that the Jewish CI uniquely survives and prospers despite persecutions and at times precisely because of persecutions or fears thereof. They are unique not fundamentally to trust immovable assets like properties or find permanent comforts in the so-called establishment but invest in intellectual assets like knowledge or crafts or invisible ties like social connections. These are ingrained in their cultural background as preference for portable assets that are difficult to be taken away. Their ruin will come about when they get rooted in the comfort and security of settled nomad. There are many other mitochondrial CIs like Huguenots in 17th century UK, US, South Africa, etc., White Russians in 20th century France, US, some even in Japan, Polish exiles in post-war UK, Australia, US, and Greeks in the US and Australia. They all brought with them knowhow, capital and connections into host countries, among which US and UK stand out as consistent with the tradition of cultural hospitality, both being the products of multi-cultures and also being nations of pragmatists.

Jewish CI is, however, most enduring in that many other mitochondrial CIs simply melted into host nationhood CIs after a few generations. The most noteworthy is the manner Jewish CI retains its strong identity. Normally, the stronger the sense of identity is, the stronger antagonism from non-members is also invited because whatever benefits they derive from a host nation they try to enclose them at the detriment of non-members, as can be seen in some Muslim communities or communities of economic refugees with cultural/linguistic isolation. Jewish CI has a core CI like its ultra-orthodox sect which demonstrates its ideological identity, which may not be shared but, nevertheless, is there for reference and tolerated by the wider CI as integral and necessary part. At the same time, offsetting this aggressive part passive members are not only left liberal but also much more dominant and internationally influential, some of them belong only subconsciously, maybe only until a critical moment. It, therefore, has a hard core and very soft shell which does less to exclude them from the world of non-members. This is the wisdom inherited from their history. I note Freemasonry CI has a similar but more intentional modus operandi in that they are a mutual-help cooperative which does its best to keep a low profile to be more effective (as can be glimpsed in 'War and Peace'). Jewish CI does this only naturally, and its almost sub-conscious looseness is a vital ingredient to be mitochondrial because to exclude is also to be excluded and does not serve well in the end neither itself nor any host CIs. On the other hand, e.g. Freemasonry CI tries to be less visible and endeavours to emphasize its charitable aspects when forced visible. Therefore, in essence, it exists to promote members' benefits at the exclusion of non-members and is, thus, seen as sinister and maybe parasitic. Purely hard core and hard skin CIs are parasitic and their sole purpose is to exploit any host CIs at the cost of non-members. They should be viewed anti-or non-social entities although some of them do little harm to the society. To these belong the likes of terrorist groups on one end and some benign religious groups on the other.

I further mention the likes of professional CIs and corporate CIs. They perform important functions within a nationhood CI providing servicing and networking. They generally constitute most of so-called economic activities. However, there are delicate balances between these subordinate CIs and the host CI in that they have their own benefits in mind while being subservient. One only has to remind oneself of e.g. the City (of London) CI which despite its contributions but, in the end, almost bankrupted the society it was to serve (Financial Crisis 07-08). Likewise e.g. the legal society CI serves the society, and it needs a certain number of members to produce good calibre ones to keep a useful standard, but too many lawyers create a dysfunctional society where social entities waste too much energy like a dog chasing its own tail suing each other, like the US lawsuit culture I might add. Therefore, a nationhood CI must have mechanism to keep balance between the interest of professional and corporate bodies and the society they serve in such a way that they do not overproduce members, who have to feed themselves for the sake of it, and who in the end harm society. Self-serving professional bodies and companies that over-sell products and services should be seen as parasitic. Many of professional services like accountancy, legal advice and representations and even medical services can be today largely substituted by IT software. This will become an inevitable trend in the foreseeable future.

Corporate activities that comprise most of our economy are often strengthened and augmented by the sense of CI. Some corporate CIs could even surpass nationhood CIs especially when the latter is weak. After all it is to feed one's mouth that one is employed, and corporations provide the jobs. However, corporations typically exploit society in order to sell products and services which the society does not necessarily need. This is where advertisements and imageries come into play to exploit the psychologies of our wellbeing, petty or otherwise. We all wish to pursue happiness, imaginary or otherwise. Corporate CIs are necessary evils as much as society needs economic activities, often simply for the sake of it. One should be aware, though, corporations exist for their sake, i.e. owners first, employees second and society a long way behind. Therefore, the propagation of corporate CIs does not always serve the interests of any higher and wider CIs. A corporate CI will seek tangencies and encompassments like any other CIs as it pursues its profits, and should be free to do so as freedom of error psychologically and logically surpasses restraints of choices. A corporate CI is, however, embedded with the destiny of self-restraints because the bigger it becomes, the more difficult to manage its sustainable growth. Only the final CI in vacuum can grow without burdens of providing benefits forever.

We should not place too much trust in the creativity or uniqueness of some CIs (nationhood or otherwise). It can be easily lost or transferred through neglect or learning. Although there is some element of cultural strength for some CI to be more creatively placed over other CIs, socio-economic forces can sometimes dismantle even cultural strength. There are many examples of lost cultures.

Finally, the more successful benefits creation is, the bigger a CI is, and the more sustainable benefits creation is, the more encompassing a CI is. A bigger CI is not necessarily more encompassing. In fact, the bigger it is beyond a certain critical point, taking into account its organization, members' ability, and bonding principles, it becomes more difficult to sustain the momentum of growth. The sustainability depends upon the availability of subjugating CIs, its structural strength and luck. Luck, as we call it, is the unfathomable nature of infinite combinations of events. A CI, which unwisely outgrew its capacity, can suddenly collapse, while a CI which, through chance or design, kept a relatively benign position can unexpectedly find a fertile ground for geometrical expansion, like the Mongol horde. However, it is safe to say that no matter what processes may take place in the progressions of CIs, it will stay within the physical boundary of available space and time.

The encompassment is always inclusive and reduces the number of CIs. If it is exclusive, then, although it may appear encompassing, it is a forced encompassment and, in fact, increases CIs. Typically, imperialism is one such example. On surface it seems to comprise of fewer CIs, but in reality suppressed CIs will surface back as ever more complex aggregates of CIs. Think of the British Empire and its aftermath. On the whole subjugating other CIs for the benefits of a host CI without really providing tangible benefits and creating a so-called empire, is a messy affair where short-term benefits are more than counter-balanced by long-term losses. Even an empire as ruthless as the Mongol Empire could not harvest benefits of today without suffering losses of tomorrow. In case of the Mongols, the temporary might of the largest and most savage empire was so easily wiped off by the empire's sudden collapse and the subsequent sufferings of its remnants. It is a way of turning a future debt into a current credit. One generation of mega-riches for a few has to be paid by many generations of an impoverished majority.

Think of the British society today. Although they pretend to be proud of their legacy, there is no denying that their society is, at least, partially negatively riddled with their imperial past, which appears to contribute non-cohesive elements in the society, at least for now. It is a small miracle that they somehow seem to contain such diverse forces within a same society and yet manage to pretend a wholeness of their CI. There will be many societies, which, if faced with the similar predicaments, will collapse, disintegrate or transform into a more selfish top-down sort of uncomfortable society, like Russia today I might add. I can easily imagine countries like China, Korea and Japan, although appear to be cohesive on surface, will find it very difficult to deal with similar dynamics, should such a situation ever arise.

Maybe the future, at some point, belongs to countries like UK and US, which have experiences of dealing with cultural, religious and racial diversities, even if not always very successfully, while maintaining traditions and momenta from the past. This is a unique strength to be reckoned with and will not be matched by any mono-cultural Far-Eastern nations, which do not have such experiences at any depths. This is how a CI learns to survive. Although an empire is gone, UK is probably the most culturally accommodating nationhood CI and provides more than passing thoughts for a higher encompassing CI. Mono-cultural strengths are turning into a future liability. Those who take an easy comfort from their security, while multi-cultural weaknesses are surfacing as social defects of various kinds, are in fact sitting on top of Pandora's box. The latter is steadily accumulating know-how and ideas to turn this weakness into strength. e.g. UK's Muslim population will contribute new contacts and knowledge (e.g. Islamic finance and laws) as 2nd and 3rd generations become more assimilated into a wider society.

Although it is not likely to be a basis for a next stage beyond nationhood CIs and is riddled with deficiencies and problems of
dealing with its imperial past, UK has magnanimousness in its culture to face diversities beyond and within its national border. This
is a rare quality to cherish and is, moreover, embedded with prov-
en track-record of dealing with such problems in a reasonably
open and transparent manner. It may produce terrorists but it is a
place these so-called terrorists want to go back to retire, once they
realize terrorism at their own peril. London is even a favorite des-
tination for Russian Mafiosi. There may be supposedly more respectable nations only because they have not had to face such diversities, they are frighteningly unproven. For any nationhood CIs
that aspire to lead a more encompassing CI, this ability to deal
with diversities is an absolute must.

The age of nationhood CIs is drawing to a close, and it is nations like US and UK that may contribute to a new CI, if not collectively (i.e. not as nationhood CIs), at cultural and infrastructural
levels, as US and UK contributed to the creativity of internet itself
as well as many new social media, not to mention great exposés of
pitfalls of these new infrastructures. I would even argue if the Nobel Peace Prize is not for those exposers, who took risks to such a
degree as to have to fear serious persecution from powerful nationhood Cis. If not for them, then maybe Nobel Prizes are already
dead institutions incorporated into the hegemonic status quo.

Considering US and UK as not only the inventors of internet
and new social media but also sources of exposés, they have a
quality of new mindsets needed for a new encompassing CI. Maybe alongside their nationhood CIs develop a borderless community administered by various like-minded creators of new media as
well as knowledgeable exposers. Thus canvassed, borderless opinions will acquire political powers and influence by maneuvering
relevant voting rights owners, given the dead-end situation of nationhood CIs and various unsavory messes they have produced in
recent years (to mention but one example, consider the illegal Iraq
war and its messy aftermaths). Call it the empowerment of disillusioned apolitical voters by social media. With hindsight our suc-

cessors will recall the Bush-Blair pair as the unscrupulous political leaders who dealt the deathblow to the history of nationhood CIs. A mediocre pair who opened the Pandora's Box which Saddam Hussein was ingenious enough to keep closed but foolish enough to be boastingly overconfident about. The victory of mediocrity over devious greed backfires as a borderless crisis which no nationhood CIs can extinguish in so far as their democracies fail to deliver undemocratic leaders.

Another reason why US and UK are likely to partake in the new CI is their stake in the English language CI supported by the widespread related entertainment and culture and extended natural allies like Canada, Australia, New Zealand and even likes of South Africa, India, Pakistan, etc. You only have to look at literature, films, popular music, sports, etc., to realize the power of English language that envelops the whole world. Whatever this new CI may be, however US and UK nationhood CIs may evolve and transmute into the new CI, the English language will play a vital role in it. Talking about US and UK nationhood CIs, the language is their biggest asset. No social media will have any global impact without the English language. Messages in English always appeal to more eyes and ears and often receive more than their fair share of influence.

Most of us are besotted with power. This comes from the necessity to provide a CI with directions. Otherwise a mere collection of individuals will not have any clues with regard to tangencies and encompassments. That is, power brings about vertical orders to a CI, and makes it possible for a CI to move about, so that it will either encompass or be encompassed. This is so ingrained in us that when there are no substances to endow power we even create false powers like so-called celebrities or keep alive long-dead empty power bases like royalties and even aristocracies. Even in these cases, fictitious powers metamorphose into degrees of money so that they will assist, in one way or another, in creating more genuine powers. Power is often manufactured by the beneficiaries.

Within an encompassing CI, other CIS are naturally encompassed by inclusion. However, there are numerous manufactured CIs, which, in one way or another, get incorporated into vertical power mechanisms and, in fact, often assist to accelerate power transmissions. These are primarily social functions of individuals seeking benefits off other individuals in a position of power or potential power. These are people who cluster around more charismatic individuals and form social units (manufactured CIs) which are more readily part of power mechanisms and benefit from being closer to power transmissions, often at the expense of other, sometimes competing, social units and outside individuals. Manufactured CIs are motivated solely by anticipated socio-economic benefits and dissipate when such benefits are found not forthcoming or exhausted. Nevertheless, such CIs have their places in the world of CIs as they too are indispensable parts of working mechanisms towards the final CI in vacuum. Typically, they explain so-called celebrities of our time, and there will be more as our world become more horizontal and become more difficult to find a place within strongly vertical mechanisms.

I even observe this in the world of academics ; e.g. a group of minor teachers of philosophy turned a clever eccentric scholar called Wittgenstein into a world celebrity and, as a result, they all enjoyed a good living as well as social respectability and managed to yield some harmless power within the pretty sordid and surprisingly unintellectual world of academic life. I even remember some cigar-smoking female professor who was a formidable debater (incidentally some professors today publicly say that is what philosophy is mainly about, i.e. narrative skills - a fitting end to Wittgensteinian era that started with the famous 'three words,' and you are better off aiming to become a barrister and listen to parliamentary debates which charge no tuition fees and are more useful, bearing all the fruits of Oxford PPE) and her husband professor of philosophy who unashamedly believed in miracles and publicly so proclaimed. In the end, even Wittgenstein danced to their tune, thinking perhaps he truly was a genius as they all said he was, and turned a bit of an old fool towards the end, flirting with religious sentiments and was surrounded by Catholic students. The latter latched on, encircled and danced around him like hyenas devouring a fame which they would never have attained by themselves, publishing his every piece of scrap and notes, writing memoirs saying he said this, he did that, he whistled beautifully, he had gay friends, etc.. What sordid characters behind posed respectability. Wittgenstein would have been a better thinker, if left alone with goats in the Austrian mountains instead of becoming a Cambridge professor. Then, we may have had a genius. I am sure you will find similar pretentious and fallacious examples of false power everywhere. Here again, messages in English language tend to have an unfair share befitting bigger audiences.

Wittgenstein famously said that "whatever can be said can be said in three words" (I count more than three words here, and I would term this as Wittgenstein's paradox; linguistic intentions and expressions do not coincide, i.e. linguistic meanings lie in the totality of that language, which has no philosophically essential relationship with linguistic mannerism. That is in the domain of art. Whatever can be said can be said in any number of words. The focus of an expression is to relate a part of language with the wholeness of that language, which will incidentally achieve a goal of art.) and made a comical *faux pas* of becoming a professor of philosophy and said considerably more than three words to say nothing really, which the old-fashioned scholar Russell ridiculed. Such is the power of a cult that people still try to see something in nothing. Wittgenstein is typically a forerunner of philosophical hippies that mushroomed in our time, who can only cant short verbalisms like cheap lawyers and do not even have Bergsonian witticism. Petty as it might be, this illustrates in some way how power allures and spoil, even for a man like Wittgenstein. Society is built around power bases, some genuine, some manufactured, some false, some imaginary, every one of which is a source of benefits for someone who lacks capacities for power. Mix them all, multiply and compound those hundred-, thousand-fold, and then you will find a source of a CI.

What applies to relatively benign academic societies applies even more acutely to mundane world of monies and businesses. Power, even false powers, is corrosive and corruptive by nature. This is necessary because orders within a CI which is dynamic and unstable by nature need to be kept reviewed and reinvented constantly in order to steer a CI, preferably, to a right direction (for the benefit creations of its members). These unpleasant characteristics of power make sure it remains itself dynamic and unstable by being repulsive to those whom it is yielded to. No power is stable, if not in space, then in time. Otherwise, there will be no tangencies and encompassments. Stability will be found only in the final CI in vacuum. Power is as unstable as CIs themselves. Power is derived and assigned within and between CIs as navigators and driving forces of tangencies and encompassments. It is also attractive as well as repulsive like a magnet. Be it the old Byzantine or contemporary England the essence is the same, although in the latter case it is better institutionalized and we use more neutral words to describe power-hunger, -struggles and -craze as if it happens naturally without personal greed.

Around so-called celebrities or false powers are cronies and parasites. Together consciously or unconsciously, they strive for better benefits, or simply to make a living, and entwined together they drip-feed more genuine power bases. This is how CIs within a CI work in real life. Taking Wittgenstein and his cronies (W-CI) as a rather trifle example it was his cronies who made Wittgenstein a world celebrity and philosophical cult which Wittgenstein surreptitiously accepted and probably enjoyed, sometimes through deliberate myths such as 'Tractatus was written in trenches of WW I' conjuring the image of the Somme and Ypres, although in reality he hardly saw any intensive actions. Through his ever increasing fame his cronies managed to have better academic and social standings as well as financial rewards, which they would not have had on their own. Many, in fact, all of his students who became professors later on were academically mediocre and philosophically barren. W-CI, with exchanges of patronage and prestige, drip-fed the fame of Cambridge University, Cambridge University in turn that of England. Be it Cambridge University or England, financially they were all better off. W-CI may be a false power, but Cambridge University and England are real powers. Compound and multiply this by hundreds or thousands from different perspectives, forms and degrees, you have a glimpse of a nationhood CI, and this is how power is manufactured and transmitted and CIs make progress. Incidentally, it was clever but ordinary Russell, part of the old establishment and a doyen of by-gone and less institutional, good, old Cambridge, who spotted Wittgenstein and afforded patronage, without which Wittgenstein would have been no more. Unlike e.g. Faraday of a century before who owes everything to none but himself, Russell himself in turn owes a great deal to the establishment for his own pre-eminence. In contrast Austria, the fatherland of Wittgenstein, benefitted practically nothing, except maybe from odd Japanese tourists mad on Wittgenstein. It is the talent of talent spotting and celebrity manufacturing, alongside the benefits of the language, that UK is particularly gifted in and at least partly explains its more than fair share in the world of culture, politics and finance. It no doubt produces geniuses, like Newton, but well mingled and camouflaged are many times more manufactured talents that were created by this unique gift and enhanced by its language and media profligate society. Here considerable PR ingenuities are deployed to create celebrities as they eventually benefit the society as a whole by invigorating its economy, which may be termed institutionally 'greedy'. Beneath the public good and charities are hidden essentially individualistic and uncaringly selfish cultures of counting coins from time immemorial, maybe because of the inhomogeneous nature of the society. Wittgenstein was exceptionally clever as well as eccentric and was a good material for a cult/celebrity status.

Celebrities are manufactured for benefit creations by petty greedy souls to lure and exploit innocents to join this artificial temporal CI. This is a top-down CI with bottom-up camouflage to benefit the inner circle, where power is based on the bonding necessities of a wider society. That is, those myriads of little artificial CIs clustered around celebrities invigorate and circulate power transmissions (mostly in the form of money) to maintain the vertical structure of a wider encompassing CI, like hemoglobin carrying oxygen. Celebrities, therefore, can only be something that is permissive by the wider CI, for destructive, disruptive celebrities will not deliver benefits to those whoever who support such celebrities, except some quirky imaginary benefits with a short life span. Good (i.e. successful) encompassing CIs encourage these little artificial CIs that do not harm them. I might call this mitochondrial symbiosis. On the other hand, bad (unsuccessful) CIs tend to supply parasitic little artificial CIs that do not invigorate the whole system. Thus, successful encompassing CIs will have harmless celebrities incorporated into the wider power structure. That is why even those celebrities who started off as social antagonists or outcasts usually turn into servants of the system as they get better off (see many pop/punk stars or villainous film stars).

In non-academic environments Machiavellian power- embodier/accumulators of various calibres are constrained within our more democratic structures by the necessity to placate public opinion. This is especially true of politicians who are not allowed ruthless pursuits of power for the sake of it. Hence, we tend to end up with mediocre politicians. Even in the world of businesses this trend applies; you may be a Machiavellian but will be forced to pretend otherwise, thus truly becoming a Machiavellian. Being trustworthy to a calculated degree is a tool of trade for anyone who pursues power and wants to build a CI. Pure science (and any academic disciplines in the idealized world) is one of a few areas one can most ruthlessly pursue power for the sake of it, for power here is, and should be, literally nothing but knowledge, and it is, and should be, irrelevant if this can be translated into money or politicized power. Such people are jewels and treasures of the humanity CI.

CIs are themselves neither right nor wrong, nor good or evil. These are the labels used in the process of encompassments for the convenience of manipulating simple souls. Seeing from the level of individual members they need benefits of a CI and they happened to be there for various factors, such as time and place, opportunities, circumstances, availabilities, etc.. It helps if they could believe, or pretend to believe, in something for the sake of bonding and more benefits. Thus some of them become proponents of a CI, some even fanatical promoters of a CI. They could easily become something else, given different circumstances or stay as they are as a result of misjudgment or for psychological ease.

Power is vertical orders needed to give a CI external directions to find tangencies and manifests as the internal strength of bonding, which depends upon its ability to create benefits for members. Benefits are created by the efficiency of working together, be it a top-down or bottom-up CI, or via discreet proxy or inner-manipulations. Increasing benefits via internal efficiency or at the expense of weaker CIs is the key to the strength and stability of a CI and the determinant factor of encompassments.

These vertical orders of transmissions are currently challenged by the appearance of social media, which make it much easier to create power horizontally and spontaneously. This is yet to be harnessed by institutionalizing the process of power creations and transmissions by carefully positioning alongside any existing power mechanisms. This will create a real democratic power which currently seems to find its place only in town squares and streets. Organizations and consequential arrangements of logistics will transform this spontaneous power into a formidable force to reckon with, which nationhood CIs have every reason to be afraid of. CIs that can harness this new power phenomenon will lead the next stage of encompassments from nationhood CIs. The social engineering of the new media has just begun, and nationhood CIs that adapt to this trend will be the winners towards the next encompassments, while those which resist or interfere will be forced to adopt at their costs. This new democratic power is powerful but we do not yet know how to harness.

Power is directional and does not permeate evenly. Quite simply if power is distributed evenly, it negates itself. Monetarily expressed (for an illustration, suitable at this stage of our history) it can only grow, and even staying still requires considerable skills and energy and means relative decline as there will be other powers that are growing and general level-up of knowledge and experience assisted by technological advances, like inflation. Thus, a receptacle of power is under constant stress to grow to test its limits and, like a CI, either encompasses (some too big and precious to fail) or is encompassed (ultimately by a tax system if fair, if not by other powers), or dies of a stroke. Power is an innate force of a CI and all the momenta of various powers are monetarily entwined to give an encompassing CI tangencies and further encompassments (remember an army marches on its stomach). As there are CIs that are not directly monetarily translatable, power and untranslatable or invisible power (like miser's fortune or buried treasure; not unnecessarily unignorable variables) comprises an encompassing CI, which itself may contain untranslatable parts.

Power is notationally the operator 'ꙍ' It is a momentum assigned to a CI by its innate necessity to form a whole, and ultimately results in Ω. Thus, it is power that logically reduces the number of CIs to end in the final CI in vacuum, where power transcends into intelligence. Power is neither good nor evil as much as CIs are neither right nor wrong. It is simplistic names given to relationships between CIs. A member of a CI may envisage any exclusive CIs as evil, and any inclusive CIs as good. Such relationships invigorate transmissions of powers, without which the process of tangencies and encompassments and the creation of the final CI will not be achieved. A CI with more inclusive encompassments is stronger, which is not too difficult in a homogeneous nationhood CI, but faces difficulties in encompassing other nationhood CIs in our world skewed towards nationhood CIs which are instinctively protective of benefits within. In this sense, EU is an experiment worth watching as a test for human intelligence. A lot is in Germany's hand.

The world of lower CIs is literally a world of power games where there will be less and less CIs and more and more power concentrated in a vertical order, to end up with a final CI in vacuum with all the power, but to yield on no one. Power metamorphoses back into a simple necessity of identifying *raison d'être*. Here the small-est, core CI with the most vivid colour coincides with the most en-compassing CI with no colour. The vertical structure that provided tangencies and encompassments collapses into the horizontal force, not of spontaneity but of sustenance. These seeming con-tradictories are accommodated because through the layers of quantifiers varying members and CIs are transformed into a uni-fied members and CIs with one and the only *raison d'être*. What makes this unity is the unity of individuals and the species. The variety and diversity of individuals and their differing pursuits of so-called 'happiness' will converge given the accumulations of our objective knowledge and through tangencies and encompass-ments of CIs. It is the eusocial destiny of life forms that forces indi-viduals to converge for the ultimate benefits of survival through space and time. At lower levels individuals and the species are overlapping because what is good for an individual is not always so for a species. At our current state of CI we do not always behave with the interest of our species at heart. Our own happiness seems different from that of our species by a very wide margin. At Ω they come to coincide.

4. The Laws of CI

The ultimate mechanism of nature is simple. There is no room for mathematical modelling and conjectural experimentations. What works, works as nature is itself mapped out according to its innate necessities. History is a trajectory of human behaviours as part of nature and comes down to the necessity of self-preservation, which creates structures of efficiencies for multiple egos to function for the purpose of the preservation of each and every ego. This necessarily results in the progression of CIs through natural selections. Although each and every ego strives to survive, it is often accidental where and how they happen to belong to a certain CI. Some CIs fail together with some members through their inefficiencies and misfortunes, some CIs lose their identity into some other CIs, while some CIs metamorphose into some encompassing CIs. Members invariably belong to more than one CI and often switch CIs according to beliefs and conveniences. A winning CI has tendencies to provide more benefits in a fairer and sustainable way.

However, CIs themselves follow simple rules. Firstly, a whole is more than the sum of parts. That is, a part or parts have an intrinsic tendency to form a whole or it is the intrinsic nature of a part or parts to form a whole, which cannot be expressed in and by the part (Hypothesis 1). This tendency or nature is 'power' and is represented by the operator '$\flat$'while ( ) represents the wholeness of a CI. Although this hypothesis is only meant for a modal logic as attempted here, it elegantly overcome problems encountered in Principia Mathematica, namely those of infinity and reducibility, which I may attempt to show separately. Put it briefly here, (x) cannot be constructed out of x, although x can be extrapolated from (x). Russell thought that a sum of parts is a sum of parts, from which a totality can be constructed by axioms pertaining from within. They (logicists) are like woodcutters who see trees, but not the forest. There are no axioms to find or construct ( ) out of x from within x. The intricacy of ( ) is not in x, but with (x). '(x) › x' is like Kantian space and time. It is a priori condition of our cognition, especially of conceptualization. Once given '(x) › x' logic will be able to generate numbers from within, which Kant thought also a priori, alongside space and time. It is not logic that is to be the foundation of mathematics, but logic and mathematics are really one and the same, and neither is to be founded on. Anyway,

$(x) › x$

,where a variable x can be any conscious entities or CIs, the simplest of which is an individual with a CI, (x), vs an individual, x. This means that a self-identified individual is more than a simple physical individual or, if applied to a CI, an encompassed CI is more than a CI in vacuum, except the final CI. The same applies to a group, thus,

$(x, y, z) › x, y, z$

,where a multiple member group, (x, y, z), is more than a mere collection of individuals, x, y, z. The expression 'more than' designates superiority, in that it is an order of nature that endows a better survival. Thus, a self-identified individual survives better than a simple physical individual and a structured CI survives better than a single CI. The same applies to groups. Furthermore,

$(x, y, z) › (x),$

where a multiple-member CI is more than a single member CI because a larger CI can afford more resources for benefits creations, e.g. like 3 small ponds made into 1 large pond, which can feed and support bigger fishes and their stocks. On the other hand, the reverse is true if a CI loses members or sub-CIs as it can happen when its bonding principles go out of fashion or become unfit for the current of a larger history.

And,

$((x)) › (x),$

where a multiple-structured CI is more than a single structured CI because an encompassment is a protective layer and adds to the strength of a CI. In general, therefore,

$(((x), (y), (z))) \rangle ((x, y, z)) \rangle (x, y, z) \rangle x, y, z \rangle x,$

where a multi-structured multi-member CI is superior to a multi-member structured CI, which, in turn, is more than a multi-member CI, which is more than a simple collection of multi-members or a single individual.

$((x, y, z))$ simply designates a layered structure and therefore can be e.g. $(x(y(z)))$ or $(x(y, z))$.

A CI is further divided into two types, where

$(z, y, x) \rangle (x, y, z),$

or, in short,

$\forall \rangle \wedge,$

which means a bottom-up CI is in general superior to a top-down CI. Thus, the most encompassing CI is $(((z), (y), (x), \cdots, (n)))$, which denotes a bottom-up multi-structured and multi-member CI. The world can be described to be moving up from a single individual to eventually an all encompassing self-identified group which consists of layers of self-identified groups where multiple members identify themselves through themselves, rather than through an inner CI.

$(\forall \rangle \wedge)$

means a metamorphosing process from $\wedge$ to $\forall$ and that more benefits are released as the inner CI loses its parasitic grips of better and more benefits to themselves at the expense of the outer CI and also as it is assimilated into the wider parametric grouping of $\forall$. On the other hand, the reverse is true if a CI metamorphoses from $\forall$ into $\wedge$ as it can happen when $\forall$ goes out of control. Thus,

$(\forall \rangle \wedge) \to e \uparrow,$

where → means a tangency. This is the benefits creations associated with the paradigm shift of a CI, where the bottom-up transformation gives rise to more benefits. The tangency of a CI in progress only refers to itself, and e stands for benefits at large, but
mainly socio-economic benefits. Thus, e ↑ or e ↓ shows its internal
process. As ($\forall$ › A) refers to a transitory state of a CI, the tangency
here means a state within, and therefore ↑ the state of increase for
benefits within and ↓ the reverse. Thus,

$(A › \forall) → e ↓,$

where benefits decrease when a bottom-up CI undergoes a
transformative change into a top-down CI for whatever reasons
because an inner CI disrupts the creations and distributions of
benefits. This is, however, an anomaly considering the meaning of
› and can only be temporary in the history of a CI simply because
of ↑ › ↓.

Referring to a CI in progress, likewise,

$((x, y, z) › (x)) → e ↑,$ and

$((x) › (x, y, z)) → e ↓$

Finally,

$(\forall (x, y, z) › A(x)) → e ↑,$

where benefits releases would be at maximum, and the reverse
of which is,

$(A(x) › \forall (x, y, z)) → e ↓,$

where benefits shrinkages would be at maximum. The examples would be e.g. a nation descending into the absolute monarch
or similar (like the current Russian state of affairs), or, as it happened to Weimar Republic a potential dictator emerging by default, through complacency and careless arrogance.

There are many shades of degrees between e ↑ at maximum
and e ↓ at maximum reflecting parametrical and quantitative
changes of a CI. One can observe many states of nationhood CIs

between the two states and maybe historically explain many falls and rises of nationhood CIs. Generally, moving from $\wedge$ to $\forall$ and concentrations of CIs will bring forth e $\uparrow$, and e $\downarrow$ will be brought about by their reverse.

The $\forall$-parametric generates e $\uparrow$ by availing a CI with the skills and talents of individuals more widely, cultivating more embracing psyche and more readily grouping with other $\forall$-parametric. The $\wedge$-parametric does the opposite in order to cater for usually corrupt and parasitic needs of the inner CI. The encompassment reduces mutually impeding CIs and make available more skills and talents of individuals who would otherwise belong to respective CIs. The break-up of any encompassing CIs will have an opposite effect. If the $\forall$-parametric and quantitative decreases in CIs due to encompassment are combined the most potent e $\uparrow$ will materialize. However, encompassments are often a structurally disruptive process and tend not bode well for the $\forall$-parametric at least temporarily.

The $\forall$-parametric grouping is a process towards an encompassing CI as deepening relationships are beneficial to all parties concerned, and as any isolated CIs suffer benefits shrinkages to the point of survival. However, the $\wedge$-parametric grouping is more of a conventional alliance because inner CIs are more concerned with benefits creations for themselves within respective CIs under their own control. If a $\wedge$-type CI should be contained in a $\forall$-grouping, then that CI needs neutering cover as it cannot behave as such without and sometimes within. The $\forall$-grouping as such further needs an extra layer of bonding that apples to only $\forall$-type CIs bar the idiosyncratic $\wedge$-type CI in order to accommodate this CI as it is forced to acknowledge the necessity of unconventional approach for the sake of benefits creations. Thus,

$(\forall (x, y, (\wedge(z)))) \, \rangle \, \forall (x, y, \wedge(z))$.

In this scenario $(\wedge(z))$ must bring an overriding benefits to counter the stress it creates. When such benefits sink to a level that is less than the benefits it brings, then $(A(z))$ is either forced out of the group or become $\forall$-transformative. Thus,

$\forall (x, y, z) \, \rangle \, \forall (x, y, (A(z)))$.

A few instances would be that US and UK were forerunners of $\forall$-parametric and quantitative changes in CIs. US started off with $\forall$-parametric and as the federal government increased its influence, especially after the Civil War and after participations in foreign warfare, its CIs became more and more consolidated and concentrated around its central government. Thus, its citizens gladly identify themselves primarily as US citizens, rather than Alabaman or Wyomingites. UK is more complex and had the dual A & $\forall$-parametric structure, in that under the imperial A-parametric its inner $\forall$-parametric was helped to consolidate and concentrate various sub-CIs into the more encompassing central CI as colonies offered plentiful opportunities to many sub-CIs, which otherwise would have squabbled and competed against each other. Besides, the deeper $\forall$-transitions within both imperial A-parametric and its inner $\forall$-parametric were relatively smooth and avoided historical accidents observed in many other countries due to national, cultural psyche typically represented by Magna Carta. US and UK are both historical recipients of e $_\uparrow$ benefits.

However, with its unique continuity of history combined with relatively healthy sense of CI UK is poised at a delicate crossroad. With the disappearance of empire and the decline of export-led economy accentuated by the unhealthy reliance on the property (of the south and London especially) and services sectors, on one hand it is reluctant to be superseded by the perceived inferior sense of CI attached to EU, on the other it is getting difficult to hold together its four little kingdoms. It is further complicated by its legacies of empire, i.e. large ethnic communities including Muslims, who are inherently indifferent or even alien to its nationhood CI, or to its culture and history. Applying the above laws of CI any divergence of CIs away from its encompassing CI will inevitably bring about e $_\downarrow$, not only to its encompassing CI but to any constituent CIs (if any left). Although EU should replace UK as an encompassing CI, the core of its CI (England) will need hard persuasions to recognize its days as an independent encompassing CI is over, maybe only after reckoning the realities of e ↓. The room for political manoeuvres and ability is already severely curtailed by the weakening of party politics brought about by the rise of horizontal forces. With it the propensity to play the deputy sheriff of the world policeman will come to halt. I must add all this was unnecessarily brought forward by the cheap populist policies of Blair. It is interesting to observe where England should be going after the full devolution and without EU, if that were to be the case. Having achieved the title of the mother of parliamentary democracy, we might as well go for the title of the father of internet direct democracy, which is inevitably in the coming. If one can file tax affairs on-line, I do not see why we should not participate in political events on-line just as easily. Party politics is in decline in many countries not by coincidences, but by horizontal forces of entrenched human rights, the new media, gender equalization, etc. People are voting not for parties of choice but for the defects of party mechanisms, so as to discourage biased policies. This is intelligent voting as against conviction voting. They are leaning to play politics with politicians and political parties. This tends to give minority kingmakers unfair advantages and makes party politics more and more distorted, awkward and unmanageable. This situation is already akin to quasi-direct democracy. It is a matter of time there come a party that advocates the internet democracy, which is a bloodless coup against proxy democracy. So England without EU and after the full devolution should go for an experimental horizontal nationhood CI, which will spearhead similar movements across the world. The alternatives will be, 1) to check the devolution and to play its full part in EU, 2) to become a middling nation, a new Switzerland of the world, where judiciary, medicine, accountancy and journalism are the main industries. For 2) to be viable, it should forget its imperial past and stop being a provider of condottieri to the world policeman (and to terrorists) and acquire more aloof but neutral colours.

It should be added here that in addition to ∀- and Λ-parametric we should be having another parametric Η (horizontal CIs) based on human rights entrenchment, etc.., and its manifestation as a sustainable horizontal force. This, however, is only a logical conjecture as Η is as yet to materialize. Historically and even theoretically, we never had any bona fide horizontal social structures, except communism in heaven. The nearest I can think of is San tribes, but these are products of extreme environments and circumstances, and only of anthropological curiosity values. Yet, Η is probably a precursory stage to Ω and a successor to ∀. Η should have the associated paradigm shift benefits and grouping. Thus,

Η › ∀ › Λ.

Both Japan and Germany experienced quantitative changes in CIs with the establishment of their modern centralized nationhood CIs and then the parametrical change from Λ to ∀, both of which brought them e ↑ benefits. Today's China underwent the radical transformation in the quality of Λ-parametric towards ∀-transitions and enjoyed a period of prosperity. However, the question posed now is whether China possesses strong and cohesive bonding principles to hold together while their nationhood CI moves from Λ to ∀. In this various horizontal forces seem to act both positively and negatively, so that the end results are by no means clear. Bear in mind what happened in the Arab Spring. The ∀-transitions could be painful and self-destructive to an undisciplined system, and that is why China is in no hurry to establish the ∀-parametric. The world is not likely to see real prosperity in China until the ∀-transitions start bearing fruits and the encompassment bring about a genuine reduction in sub-CIs, i.e. until the so-called communist party is replaced by all democratic multi-party system.

The process of encompassments and tangencies is dynamic and fluid and it is this unstable but directional conditions that form history. As time passes, there will be fewer and fewer CIs. Socio-economic units move up from smaller and numerous to larger and fewer CIs, so e.g. family CIs, tribe CIs, etc. are replaced by clan CIs, kingdom CIs, etc.., and currently predominated by nationhood CIs and multi-national corporate CIs, which are being woven into a world string by cross-border networking via the new media.

However, the biggest challenge we face is not this dynamic process. Over whatever individual misfortunes and difficulties all CIs will eventually converge and metamorphose into an all encompassing CI and it is this final CI that poses an intellectual dilemma to us all. This happens because at this CI there are no benefits to be derivable. Benefits are derivable because in the dynamic encompassing process lesser CIs are always in a state of conflict where some win at the expense of others, much like some individuals win over others for various reasons such as intelligence, physical strength, mental agility, etc.. Benefits are winners' spoils over losers whether at individuals' level or at CIs' level. There are no winners without losers. With no other CIs, inner or outer, the universal and even CI is in vacuum and cannot enhance members' benefits. Here, all members are equal and there are no other CIs to conquer, like evenly distributed power. In this state, therefore,

$$\Omega \succ \sim\Omega,$$

where Ω represents the final encompassing CI in vacuum. The final CI, Ω, faces the simple choice of 'to be or not to be' with the obvious answer. This is possible only with the paradigm shift from the love of self, which is the driving force of the lesser CIs, to the selfless love of life, which extends to all forms of life, the earth-bound or otherwise, assuming this logic of modality across the universe. Unless we come across alien life forms contrary to this modality, Ω is the final CI. Otherwise, Ω becomes the earth CI surrounded by non-earth CIs and the process of encompassing can go on. The mission of the earth CI is to preserve the earth life form, while the mission of Ω is to preserve any life forms assuming all life forms share the same logic of modality.

After reaching the final CI, the lack of motives to win over other individuals or CIs needs the transcendence of life from competitions to tranquil contents. I further extrapolate that without needs for tangencies and encompassments Ω is horizontal by structure and nature, and towards the final process it is not the confrontational vertical power structure that bring about Ω, but the 'horizontalization' of CIs in the latter stages of the evolution of CIs that together generates Ω. So the paradigm shift from $\forall$ to H together with H grouping will replace tangencies and encompassments at these latter stages of CI evolution. Nationhood CIs will not suddenly disappear as if by revolution, rather it is their gradual transformation from vertical to horizontal power structure that gives rise to the paradigm shift towards Ω. The reason why this is an intellectual challenge is that we have never historically experienced the stage of Ω, neither do we know much about horizontal power structures. Be it superego or categorical imperative, history was so far always propelled not by some high moral principles dreamt by scholastic speculations, but by pools of blood, by the necessities of power, often ending up filling the stomach of a few at the expense of nameless multiples. All too often we play games and enjoy playing games, be it politics, businesses or emotional games. Sometimes, it is games themselves that matter, not even consequences. This lower end of intelligence is what makes life exciting and contradicts intellectualism.

Given the minimum to sustain ourselves physically, which is not too difficult in our time of plenty, it is this game playing mentality of ours that seeks problems for the sake of problems. For those who are not fit or good to play games there are those others who become professionals to play games or provide games. It was Roman politicians' predominant roles to provide so-called citizens with endless games of no useful productivity. See how every provincial Roman town was endowed with an amphitheatre and gladiators were celebrities of the day. Likewise, it is a major part of our economy to provide games, quasi-games or related products and services to consumers. If you include politics, diplomacies, financial trading, etc., as games, in fact any human transactions, then our world centres on games. It is as if intelligence is embedded with a necessity of self-degeneration in order to prevent it from flying too high. Intelligence is deployed for most of us to maximize

happiness with least efforts. Happiness has a variance of id to superego depending upon preference and necessities, but for great
majority of humans it is generally a transitory emotional state of
petty sorts.

Thus, for intellectualism intelligence is a necessary condition,
but for intelligence intellectualism can even be an idiosyncratic
diversion. Given $\Omega \rangle \sim\Omega$ as a logical consequence it is the task of Ω
that unites intelligence with intellectualism. Ω is in vacuum and
seeks no tangencies or encompassments. If its survival is not to be
left to chances, intellectualism and intelligence must work in tandem and it is the only function of the final CI, of which the only
benefit is the survival of life form.

Finally, a psychotic state of affairs is a quasi-final CI, hence in
pseudo-vacuum and seeks neither tangencies nor encompassments. This is so because there can be no totality in contradiction.
No whole can be found in two exclusive states of affairs. A wholeness of a state of affairs and its own negation is a logical break-
down with reality. Thus, denoting this quasi-final state of affairs as
Ψ,

$$(\Psi \wedge \sim\Psi)$$

represents the most extreme form of a psychotic CI (quasi-CI).
A psychotic CI results when exclusive CIs fail to have an encompassment. Members then belong to two CIs without conciliatory
encompassment. It should be noted that two exclusive CIs can coexist if only they can be encompassed, i.e. if only there is an encompassing CI through which members of each CI can benefit by
so coexisting. A psychotic CI is similar to the final CI in the sense
that it has no more tangencies and encompassments and is in vacuum. It is, however, not a whole that has parts and any attempt to
make tangencies and encompassments are in vain.

Psychotic CIs, therefore, have difficulties of various degrees or
inability to form a whole and are short of, or lack, the capacity of
tangencies and encompassments. This may apply from one member with or without CI to multi-member CIs of higher encompass-

ing level. The most extreme form of a psychotic CI is the schizo-phrenic CI. These generally start from a normal CI, usually top-down form, as reality checks are less likely to be performed at top-down CIs than bottom-up CIs. Bottom-up CIs are generally more censured by more members and although they tend to be less effi-cient, they are more stable. The general form of psychotic CI is $(\Psi \wedge {\sim}\Psi)$. It should be noted that $(\Psi \wedge {\sim}\Psi)$ is not the same as $\Psi \wedge {\sim}\Psi$ because $\Psi \wedge {\sim}\Psi$ per se is not able to form a whole. At $(\Psi \wedge {\sim}\Psi)$ a state of affairs is a failed and dysfunctional CI centred on a split or con-tradictory identity which seek tangencies and encompassments where no reconciliations can be found. It is this infertile attempt that is called mental illness. This applies to individuals as well as to institutions. Their reality is their own failed CI centred on falla-cious wholeness away from the reality of other CIs, hence in pseu-do-vacuum.

Fanatical religious CIs and fascist political CIs are examples of this type. They are in the end more nuisances than bona fide threats, although our politicians like to emphasize their danger and that they could cause serious damages. The lack of their ability for tangencies and encompassments limits the extent of their in-fluence and thereby their existence. As soon as they burn them-selves out in an attempt to seek tangencies, they tend to fizzle out as members switch identity or exit surreptitiously and as they lack a whole to be catastrophically explosive. Consider the world where everyone is fanatical and fascist. It would not be long before the call for common sense is summoned from within. The most practi-cal way of dealing with psychotic CIs is the awareness of more tan-gible benefits elsewhere or within themselves via different routes and the provision of wider knowledge, rather than outright con-frontations.

We are ingrained with respect for power, which represents the hierarchical nature of a CI (except Ω). A CI is of necessity hierar-chical because, proxy democracy or otherwise, without a vertical order no CIs can establish a direction to move forward, be it a deci-sion making or an administrative process. This, however, now faces a new paradigm. With the proliferations of the social media, human rights, etc.., CIs are hypothetically in a position to have a collective decision, dispensing with hierarchical necessity. CIs can be made directional collectively, spontaneously and simultaneously with a proper institutionalization of the social media. This new ability of CIs will change our perception of power. Power need not be represented by persons or hierarchical positions. It is a CIs itself that is immediately transmissive. Politicians will do their utmost to resist this depersonification of a CI as they will lose their power base and be taken over by less privileged social media administrators.

I distinguish 'force' from 'power.' 'Power' has a vertical structure which expresses itself as tangencies and encompassments. 'Force' is less structural and manifests itself horizontally so to speak. It impacts power and influence momentum of tangencies and encompassments. It is not easy to harness 'force' because of its spontaneity. If 'force' should destroy 'power' without a replacement CI, then it has to go through painful transformations of establishing a CI out of itself. The process can be brutal because 'force,' left alone, has to search for a CI in simpler and more primitive ways. Here tangencies and encompassments centre on the strength to survive, without which no benefits will be forthcoming. Out of the chaos of 'force' it is the strength of bonding, not individual strength of will, tactics or intelligence, that surfaces as an encompassing CI. It is only at Ω 'force' become synonymous with 'power' as there is nothing any more to encompass.

CIs progress into the final CI in vacuum because a whole is also a part once so formed until the all embracing whole is reached.

$$\Omega \rightarrow (((x))) \rightarrow (x(y(z))) \rightarrow (((x), (y(z))) \rightarrow ((x), (y), (z)) \rightarrow (x), (y), (z) \rightarrow x, y, z$$

The all-embracing whole is either itself or nothing.

$$\Omega \rightarrow \sim\Omega$$

To start with, a CI is a common identity which encompasses isolated group entities, and without which those entities are less efficient in terms of benefits creation. This is a symbiotic communality which catalyzes benefits creation into a whole that is more than the sum of simple parts. That is, more benefits are derived from an entity where members are aware of social bonds amongst themselves. Thus;

(x) › x,

where (x) is a CI with a group entity of 1 member, while x is a simple individual. The extension of this is;

(x, y, z) › x, y, z,

where (x, y, z) is a CI with a group entity of 3 members, while x, y, z are simple individuals and z extends to n, which is an optimal number appropriate to the group structure of (x, y, z). The extension of this is;

(x (y (z))) › ((x), (y), (z)),

where (x (y (z))) is a fully encompassing CI with 3 group entities, while ((x), (y), (z)) is a CI with 3 sub-CIs, and ( ) designates a wholeness. Likewise, z extends to n. Here, in terms of the power of benefits

creation;

(x (y (z))) › ((x), (y), (z)) › (x, y, z)

That is, a CI is more embracing and powerful if it has more members, and moreover if it has more sub-CIs. Above all;

Ω › (x (y (z)))

This is an optimal CI where it embraces (x) which in turn embraces (y) which embraces (z). This multi-layered, all-embracing CI does not react with any other CIs (and hence (((x)))) and therefore its benefits are simply its own existence, which dynamically manipulates all its layered CIs in such a way as to promote their existence. Thus;

Ω › ~Ω

Given an optimal CI with an optimal number of members in such a way that all members are embraced, the sole and only benefit derivable is the preference for survival.

The above is a schematic representation kept as simple as possible, but a more complex system can be easily built by introducing various modal operators. This more complex system may be correct at a point in time and place. However, social modality is fluid and is over time likely to change shape and colour time and time again. I shall expand the above schematic representation into a slightly more complex explanatory system by using simple operators, inclusive, overlapping and exclusive, and further, a quantifier to designate strength. Thus, a system of CIs with more inclusive CIs is stronger, while that with more exclusive CIs is weaker, and at the weakest point it can be described schizophrenic. Let us consider 3 member CI for a simplicity's sake. The strongest system, for example, consists of a dot like CI of the ego (id measured against a society) encircled by a CI which is a biological bond, contained in a CI which socially incorporates the middle CI. Thus;

which is identical with (x (y (z))). This is the schematically strongest CI that consists of 3 members. It is, for example, self supported by its biological relations who belong to a society with which they share a same destiny and form a good fighting unit, like a chief and his family leading a tribe. The core CI, the middle CI and the outer CI share the same benefits; what is good for one is good for all. This CI is described to be all-inclusive. If this CI can develop into a n-member CI by adopting ever wider embracing CIs, then the resultant group is coherently inclusive for all members at all levels. However, the fringe CI is often maintainable only in a non-vacuum condition, i.e. only as opposing to some other CI. Therefore, this CI is ultimately exclusive and in itself self-destructive. It is in the process of forming an ever larger CI that gives a temporary appearance of all-inclusiveness.

On the other hand;

$(x \, \rangle \, (y \mid z))$

This is the weakest of 3-member CI, where two exclusive members belong to the same CI. It is e.g. a tribe which contains two mutually exclusive leading families or the mirthless union of Tito's Yugoslavia. This CI is described as half inclusive. The 2 core CIs share benefits only to the extent that not doing so endangers their existence, that only the bare minimum liaison is needed for the embracing CI. For example, usually exclusive religious groups may unite for the convenience of opposing a totally non- or anti-religious force, like a jihad that suspends all personal and tribal feuds, united by a common enemy. Or two unfriendly nations may form a united front to fight a regime which threatens them both, as e.g. USSR and US did against Nazi Germany in the nominal name of the allied forces. One would observe the meaning of 'perfidious Albion' here. Once again, the embracing CI is maintained only in a non-vacuum condition. CI with the only constituent of self may exist in vacuum in some circumstances, otherwise it always presupposes other CIs inclusively, exclusively or overlappingly. This is so because identity is readily establishable against other identities, and because a CI has to be simple and easy to be shared by multiple individuals. This CI disintegrates into more inclusive CIs as soon as the embracing CI disappears because of the lack of opposing or surrounding CIs.

Thus, if the 2 exclusive CIs should lose the common destiny to unite them for any reasons, then this 3-member CI is the same as;

$(y) \mid (z)$

Two CIs without any embracing CI is schematically the same as a single unrelated CI. It should be noted that if they are related in terms of exclusion, there has to be an embracing CI which derives benefits out of this exclusion. That is, exclusion *in situ* is an inter-

action that benefits both parties for being so. Otherwise, their relation will develop into inclusion or overlap. Therefore,

$$\bigcirc | \bigcirc$$

y, z,

where | stands for exclusion, is the same as $\bigcirc$. One might con-
sider

$$\bigcirc \| \bigcirc$$

y, z,

where it may be termed as mutual exclusion. CIs, generally, by
being excluded, also exclude and, therefore, the unilateral exclusion is the same as mutual exclusion by implication, although pro-
cess-wise there may be some subtle difference. In terms of the
scheme here, they are both the same as,

$$\bigcirc$$

y

Then one might consider overlapping CIs. Thus;

$(x \, {}^{,} \, ((y)(z)))$

For example, male CI and female CI are overlapping, rather
than exclusive because, on one hand, both CIs belong to a common larger CI, namely human CI and accompanying communal
benefits, on the other, some benefits are derived from, and enhanced by, their respective CI. This dynamic relationship between
the two CIs, however, weakens the embracing CI because it is often
volatile and sometimes negative. That is, a CI that contains overlapping CIs is inherently less stable than an all-inclusive CI and is

therefore weaker. If one is to identify oneself as belonging to e.g. human CI via e.g. female CI, this is inherently weaker than simply identifying oneself as belonging to human CI. This is so because the overlapping part, i.e. male CI positively or negatively interferes with the overall identification in a way that averages out less than the straightforward identification.

Therefore, given all CIs are eventually to come under one CI, overlapping CIs are rather a process for encompassment. Overlapping CIs, as they are, cannot develop into a higher embracing CI from within themselves. They are rather encompassed by another CI via knowledge and education and within this encompassing CI they are doomed to be absorbed into a higher CI. That is, like exclusive CIs, which without an encompassing CI turn into unrelated CIs, therefore into a schematically independent single CI, overlapping CIs and exclusive CIs are therefore eventually transformed into encompassing CIs.

Three laws of CI are derived from Hypothesis 1. To reiterate (x) is a CI, whereas x is an individual. (x) is more than x. The first law is that a CI is more (stronger) than an individual. Likewise, (x, y, z) is an organizational CI, whereas x, y and z are members. The second law is that an organizational CI is more (stronger) than a simple CI. This is so because members derive more benefits from an organization, i.e. benefits are more tangible and stable. Organizations have more tangencies with other CIs and individuals and therefore can derive more benefits through encompassments. The third law is that ((x), (y), (z)) is more (stronger) than (x, y, z). That is, an encompassing CI is more (stronger) than an independent CI as the former is structurally more coherent than the latter. The layers of ( ) are the quantifier to designate the strength of CI. An encompassing CI that went though the process of more encompassments is intrinsically more (stronger) than one with less encompassments. Thus, through encompassments identities may be dynamically passed and absorbed into a higher CI where each process is inherited as strength. The all-encompassing CI is a single CI with highest quantifiers, and since there are nothing more to encompass it is in vacuum. Ω is, therefore, synonymous with $(\cdot \ (\cdot \ (x)))$.

At Ω it is not tangible benefits that bond members, but it is the strength of identity as established through layers of encompassments. Benefits permeate evenly and we do not compete or strive to negate each other's ability to gain and amass more benefits as we seem engaged for most of our mental capacity today. Such benefits and identity are intellectual.

The final CI in vacuum is a non-vertical power. It therefore has no tangencies and encompassments. For horizontal forces to metamorphose into a horizontal power, it cannot have any moving parts as they immediately form a vertical structure in order to form a whole. Parts must instantly equate a whole, and this can only be an intellectually transformed totality or merged mind. I am not sure if we are ever able to achieve such a totality. Still we have a vast room to evolve, and remember minds are merging into a single entity through internet entanglements. If we do not, then artificial intelligence will take our place, post singularity. Relating to Ω power negates itself if evenly permeated (Hypothesis 2). Power is a tool to achieve a whole from part(s) through tangencies and encompassments. As Ω is in vacuum and there are nothing to encompass, power here has no *raison d'être*.

Likewise, money, which is the socio-economic expression of power, bases its value on uneven distributions. As a tool to govern our society, money empowers people and organizations to seek directions towards consolidations. That is, power and money are expressions of vertical differentials in humans and CIs. Like heat death of the 2nd law of thermodynamics power loses its usefulness as it permeates more and more evenly. In a society in which everyone is well-off by right, it will become more and more difficult to manoeuvre people or organizations to any designated direction. It also follows that the presumed spontaneous and horizontal forces due to the new media, human rights, etc.., has no vertical basis for power or any of its derived entities such as money.

Ω must therefore exist without vertical power structures, which is almost alien to our comprehension of human history, cultures and societies. Except for some idealised social theories like communism in heaven, it is pragmatically taken for granted that none of us are equal and depending on our abilities, capacities, deeds and will benefits are obtained and distributed reflecting such differences, and it is up to individuals to utilize benefits as such depending on their needs, be they psychological, political, socio-economical, biological, etc. Even San tribes have some vertical structure based on ageism. There are some signs such as the entrenchments of human rights, waves of horizontal forces from the new media and intelligent voting to discourage party politics, etc.., that point to the direction of a horizontally networking CI (tentative directions towards a more horizontalized CI can also be seen in 'blockchain' , 'distributed ledgers,' 'bitcoin,' 'shared ownership communities,' 'citizens' basic income,' etc..). Whatever it may be, it will need a large dose of intellectualism and less of greed-based mindsets, the reverse of which is more or less our current norm.

The dynamism of history provided by the process of tangencies and encompassments will no doubt propel us to a stage not known to us now. Like motion, which cannot be broken down to a divisible line, self is an ever-constant present in motion, the momentum of which indicates the past and the future. The momentum of self is a circle of identity, which our ego adopts for its material survival, convenience and psychological benefit with varieties allowed for catering for intellectual tastes and calibres. Cultures, religions, education, wealth, politics, etc., provide many different circles of identity. However, the prime purpose of adopting one is to safeguard one's survival. Continua of present with momentum from the past and the biological dictum of the future overcome space-time constraints and biological limitations. It is our will to survive that forces us to graduate from blind alleys of nationhood CIs and guide us to a next stage of CI.

History is as much made of fictions as there are different descriptions of the same object and event. It is for this reason that the history of ideas is a superior form of historical description to a narrative history. Even then, one can never be sure with any certainty of the value of one interpretation over another. The idea of progressive encompassing CI takes events as a flux, and a CI itself is a

colourless concept except that the ultimate benefits to bind us together is to (try to) survive over space and time. The laws of CIs
describe tools of evolutions of CIs, which culminates in Ω.

Benefits that bond us started off with tangible, socio-economic
benefits but metamorphosed into a benefit of rather metaphysical
existence and survival. It is easy to reconcile them at an individual
level where we experience from id to superego in one life span and
in one body and mind and we (more or less) remain one identical
self regardless. However, CIs are conventions fit at each stage of
human developments and evolutions. Unlike us CIs do not retain
one self after metamorphoses and, thus, transform into another CI
after encompassments. Where nationhood CIs look decidedly
dominant it may appear supercilious to any other possibilities of
CIs. It is only with the consideration for the ultimate purpose of
our existence that we recognize nationhood CIs are another convention fit for a time and place of the way we manage our destiny
to the best of our ability.

We enjoy our life and look forward to the future only because
we rightly or falsely self-assure ourselves of an eternal linear trajectory of our history. However, the indulgent fact that we see no reasons to think otherwise is no guarantee there is a tomorrow. As a
matter of physics as it stands today, we do not have any tomorrow,
given the time scale of millions instead of hundreds. It is perhaps
our psychological safety mechanism not to think beyond our tangible individual selves, but we die as individuals and maybe as
species. Ω will come as our last stand to survive, perhaps sooner
than anticipated.

At Ω we have no vertical power structures, no vertically divergent socio-economic benefits. The overriding benefit is our intellectual unity to (try to) survive over the odds of space and time.
Maybe artificial intelligence is closer to the essence of Ω, if only it is
embedded with the ability to produce idiosyncratic geniuses.
Meanwhile, we are here to guide, protect and lead artificial intelligence as long as we can or are allowed. Thereafter, we assist and
live alongside, once again as long as we are useful. That is, unless

we can shed our animal skins and metamorphose into more intellectual, thinking machines instead of being players of games.

Nationhood CIs are showing signs of fatigue after two or three hundreds years of wear and tear. The amount of waste of resources (materials and intellectual) owing to nationhood CIs even as we speak does seem to point to the possibility that it is past its sell-by date. It follows from one of the laws of CI that we search for a new encompassing CI to replace nationhood CIs. As mentioned elsewhere, it will probably come from the 'horizontalization' of CIs due to the entrenchments of human rights, the new media, the collapse of party political systems and gender equalization.

There are many more stages of encompassments to follow nationhood CIs before we reach Ω, and it will be amusing to pontificate what they might be. Although it is not too speculative to imagine what the immediate next stage may be, one might be entering the world of fictions and science fictions thereafter. Logic only dictates the process of tangencies and encompassments for less and less CIs and to eventually reach Ω. Meanwhile the dynamics of processes at play, numerous variables, various contingencies and possibly catastrophes will impact actual outcomes of encompassments. I leave those for my Sunday dreaming, and skipping the intermediate CIs I finally mention the intellectual purposes of Ω:

Supposition 1: Life forms appear anywhere and anytime in the universe given certain physical conditions and evolve into universally identical intelligent beings. If this is the case, there is nothing special in being humans and therefore we have no privileged purposes to strive as an individual and as a species. Whatever we achieve, will be also achieved somewhere and sometime in the universe. However, it is imperative to know and definitively confirm that this is indeed the case. If only it is, then we are just a phenomenon and as such we should spend our life in an epicurean manner in a philosophical sense. But, here without a higher dimension ethics is essentially a name for social conventions to equilibrate maximum individual benefits and our forced mutual existence, without too much stresses for either.

The key to happiness here is good sleep, good poo and good food everyday at minimum costs and to cultivate mind to enjoy balanced peace within and without. Although we may be too hypocritical to admit this, this is more or less what the wiser among us strive for today.

Supposition 2: Life forms on earth are unique and bear an earth signature. This is called Earth Logic. These earthly life forms evolve into earthly intelligent beings, given certain physical conditions. What we achieve on earth, only we can achieve. If this is the case, we have a duty to preserve an earthly life form. Our long-term goal is to make sure earthly achievements and earthly life forms survive any cosmic catastrophes. This is the purpose of our existence.

The key to happiness here is to achieve the maximum knowledge that allows us such preservations. The society should be engineered to produce as much objective knowledge as possible.

Supposition 3: Human beings are unique not only on earth and but also in the universe. Whatever we achieve, only we can achieve. The purpose of our life is to strive as an individual and as a species to achieve our maximum potential. Our goal is to preserve our achievements and human life form through any cosmic catastrophes. We should be able to maintain our biological identity and overcome any physical limits imposed on us via space-time continuum.

Ethics here is knowledge is everything and we should plan to balance needs of individuals and necessities of species in a way to maximize knowledge productions. Although knowledge is as important as in Supposition 2, it is more challenging as we need to maintain our biological identity through cosmic catastrophes.

A solution to these 3 suppositions is the key to our intellectual happiness and fulfilment of our existence as individuals and as a species. Everything else such as our socio-economic and political activities, scientific endeavours apart from the pursuits of these suppositions directly or indirectly, any other intellectual and artistic deeds are important but secondary. Meanwhile, we are still far away from even knowing where we may stand in such pursuits.

My own feelings go for Supposition 2 as it is rather sad to think of Supposition 1 as our goal. We as a life form are nothing special, but we may represent an earthy life form, which probably may not be unique in the universe. However, it must be exceedingly gratifying to know if the form of human intelligence is the form of intelligence regardless of its origin. If this is the case, Supposition 2 sadly moves on to become Supposition 1, but it will be a long time to find that out, and all 3 Suppositions by necessity share a same path until we establish if there are other life forms elsewhere in the universe and if any intellectual forms share a same basis, i.e. logic and mathematics. Supposition 3 is too narrow for my likings, and I fear this is almost a new religion for pseudo scientific characters.

My personal belief is as follows:

Existence is description. The structure of existence is the structure of description and is necessarily schematic. Human existence is a description only as much as any existence is a description and is placed at an equal platform to any other existences. This is so because in the schema of life forms the only raison d'être is the existence (survival) of life form in its widest sense. Given any forms of life, it will eventually evolve into some sorts of intelligent life form, and intelligence as perceived in human life form has no claim to be the domineering form of intelligence in so far as the human existence has no guarantee to last in the present form or in any forms. If human life form has not found a way out to survive by the time our physical environments become too challenging, we will do less well than the most primitive bacterial life form in terms of the cosmic survival games. Besides, considering how little we managed to know, it is highly questionable that human intelligence should be the only criterion in this human preference of the vertical presentation of the schema of life. At the end of day, whether it is intelligence or primitiveness that saves life forms from cosmic catastrophes, is unknown and moreover it is likely that given certain conditions any life forms will eventually acquire so-called intelligence and may even provide a better understandings of life, universe and everything. Hitherto intelligence only proved to be a double-edged sword (most ironically observed in Fritz Haber, who contributed in the invention of explosives and fertilizers through Haber-Bosch process, who gave us a heaven (abundant foods) and a hell (unlimited ammunitions, not to mention Zyklon A) simultaneously and, therefore, to whom we owe both war and peace, and most interestingly he was a Jew). Although there may have been some progress in accumulating practical knowhow of how to exploit material environments, in any deeper sense of knowledge one should feel awed how little we really come to know.

Intelligence, whatever it may be, has no special privileges in terms of understanding. Existence is description and therefore the manifestation of understanding. Humans cannot claim any special standing because of intelligence and have no right to interfere with other life forms. Should we ever come to escape into space, we will be sending as our representative either the most primitive earthy life form or the artificial intelligence as culmination of human intelligence in the hope it will either eventually evolve into intelligent earthly life forms given certain physical conditions or propagate itself in a self-replicable form.

5. Types of CI

The primary purpose of a CI is to safeguard members' interests against any other CIs not contained in an immediate encompassing CI. While the laws of CI predict the encompassment as the natural evolution of CIs, to result in an over all encompassing CI, which is in vacuum, the process is itself dynamic caused by types of members and of CIs as well as relations between CIs. This dynamic and fluid process is what I would like to call history.

Λ (top-down) and $\forall$ (bottom-up) are parameters as every CI is necessarily either of them, while h (human rights) is a constant, applicable to every CI. h is not a CI but could contribute towards the humanity CI by levelling nationhood CIs and other vertically orientated CIs, given a sustainable structure with benefits without vertical power transmissions.

Λ and $\forall$ are schematically $\Lambda \lor \forall$ as every CI is either Λ or $\forall$. However, in reality there are many shades of interchanges as CIs are flexible and dynamic. It is only for schematic illustrations every CI can be affixed with Λ or $\forall$. h is a constant that restrains vertical power structures because members of a CI cannot be fully subject to vertical power transmissions when assigned with h. That is, h is a horizontal force, a leveller, which protects members from limitless transgressions of vertical power that is needed to sustain a CI. h is transformed into a parameter H (for horizontal CIs) when $\forall$ is horizontalized. Fully horizontalized $\forall$-CIs tantamount to a single H-CI, which is identical with Ω.

Λ, $\forall$ and h are illustrated to be related as follows,

$$\Lambda / h^2 = \forall / h,$$

where Λ requires twice more restraining force of h as needed by $\forall$. Λ is slow to act on the demand of h as they tend to have a CI within a CI and its inner CI is more isolated, i.e. h has to be doubly applied, and therefore its downfall can be more dramatic than $\forall$. $\forall$, on the other hand, can more easily placate h by being more sensitive to the demand of h and by subtly camouflaging the vertical nature of its power. Nevertheless, h could have a metamorphosing influence over $\forall$. That is, horizontal forces as represented by h often appear destructive or disruptive especially seen from vertical power transmission mechanisms. This applies more so to Λ than to $\forall$ because Λ is more for the benefits of the inner CI and heavily relies on the hierarchical presentation of the will of a few. Therefore, in order to achieve a similar influence larger h is required and accordingly tends to effect more drastic results. However, what appears destructive can also be creative, especially for $\forall$, because $\forall$ is more adoptive and transformative to accommodate horizontal forces if they are sufficiently large. See how some nationhood CIs so readily changed their characteristics, or even national psyche, to facilitate women's suffrage, gay rights, and feelings of religious or racial minorities, etc.., in recent years.

The cold war was as much a war of ideology as a war between Λ and $\forall$, which still remains unresolved. If it were a matter of ideology (even then so-called communism was never much more than a tool of governance and only initially a bonding principle), then with the disappearance of USSR Russia would have ceased to be a military threat. This is apparently not the case, with their nuclear capacity intact and their energy and foreign policies treading on the old imperial ambitions. Much the same applies to China. They heavily rely on the Λ-model because they are based on a socio-economic model where a CI has to be forced on, rather than instilled in, the majority. That is, their nationhood CI is not based on equity shares of benefits to be earned together, but rather benefits to be distributed (of course, after the appropriation by the inner CI).

Λ-CIs are more resilient to h and give the impression of political strength as the decision-making is shorter and simpler primarily to reflect the self-interests of the inner CI. However, this prima facie strength is brittle as it only represents the benefits of the inner CI ultimately at the expense of the outer CI and, thus, intrinsically abhors ħ. Since Λ-CIs are more political by nature and more vertically orientated by modus operandi, they are not really fit socio-economically. It is only at a time of strong growth that the interests of the inner- and outer-CIs appear superficially coincided as many contradictions and conflicts can be temporarily ignored. In addition, no matter how strong a Λ-CI may appear at times, since this strength depends so much on so few, it is inevitable it is not easy to get over the tests of time.

Λ-CIs are inherently unstable because of their not necessarily consistent dual structure and, thus, have an inclination to externalize their inner inconsistencies, typically playing a nationalistic card, e.g. Ukraine, Crimea, East- and South-China seas, etc. Historically they positively look for, or even create, external problems so as to redirect the eyes of the outer CI from internal concerns to external problems. Contemporary examples are easy to find in Putin, Xi, North Korea, etc.. Being a passive member in a Λ-CI will bring least benefits as the inner CI takes precedence in benefits sharing. The inner CI, therefore, needs placating these highly useful outer passive members by continuous propagandas and disinformation in the form of top-down nationalism. This creates the undercurrent of tensions and stresses. The only exception is bottom-up nationalism (e.g. Napoleon France), where spoils of war are plentiful to satisfy even less privileged members, at least temporarily, and thereafter in the glow of memories.

The reverse is more or less true for ∀-CIs. Their strength is their simpler and consistent structure as a CI which is, in theory, not subject to any controlling or manipulating minorities. The interests of a ∀-CI are also the interests of all its members and therefore every member is also an equity stake holder. Although in reality there are shades of controlling or manipulating interests here and there, they are well-disguised enough not antagonize the majority and quick to realign when faced with uncomfortable disclosures because their stakes are not really a matter of life and death, and their wealth and security depend so much on the society in which they also live.

Apart from Λ and $\forall$, there are many types of CIs which are not parametrical but simply characteristics of CIs. To name but a few; e.g. special purpose CIs such as 'feminists,' 'gay rights,' 'religious,' 'political,' 'animal rights,'or even 'gardening or book clubs,' etc.., mitochondrial CIs such as 'reciprocating minorities' and parasitic CIs such as 'exclusive minorities.'

Special purpose CIs are to protect, promote and propagate the benefits of members of specific bonding principles. The most outstanding and successful example would be nationhood CIs at their conception. They, however, have been so successfully encompassing that they now form a global superstructure where nationhood CIs mutually guarantee each other's existence by wide margin of tolerance (sovereignty). They almost completely dominate the world in terms of legality and finance as they have domineering enforcement powers. Thus, because of the interlinked state of mutual guarantees, also via common marketplaces shared through corporate CIs as well as the shared parameter ($\forall$) nationhood CIs are no longer special purpose CIs but tools of the stalemate infrastructure aptly named 'nationhood mutual guarantee scheme'. By the laws of CIs this cannot last as one of the most fundamental principles of CIs is encompassment, which cannot be blocked until Ω is reached. The emergence of more and stronger horizontal forces will once again rekindle the tangency and encompassment process. The only nationhood CI (US) that was endowed with the potential of metamorphosing into a higher encompassing CI seems to have missed that precious momentum for her inability to shed the shell of a nationhood CI. It is, thus, that some run of the mill historian call it the end of history, although this is in fact the beginning of a new era to search for a new CI to graduate from nationhood CIs. US's benefits from $\forall$-grouping are capped by its nationhood status and now should aim for H paradigm by taking an initiative. China will not benefit from $\forall$-grouping unless it shifts from $\wedge$ paradigm.

One of special purpose CIs, 'Muslim community' at large deserves some consideration. Although a finger is pointed at them for a responsibility for the so-called radicalization,it was ultimately the responsibility of an adopting society for failing to make Muslims an equity partner of the society that some started to use the religion as the front of a respectability to express their antisocial reactions. A society, once adopted a minority group, by debts from imperial pasts, by policy errors or by economic necessity or legal obligations, is responsible to fully incorporate them, and they have legal rights to, into the mainline society. A minority group often retains its exclusive characteristic as a reaction to being marginalized and not given full access to enjoy socio-economic benefits. A society should not adopt any minority groups if it is not fully prepared to encompass it, and once having adopted for whatever reasons, it is in the benefits of the wider society to integrate it at any costs because it will sooner or later incur larger costs for not doing so, especially for $\forall$-CIs. Be it Huguenots, Jewish or Polish émigrés, after 1 or 2 generations they fully integrated into the host society, I do not see why the same cannot be done for Muslims, given every opportunity to develop socio-economically.

Mitochondrial CIs are symbiotic in the sense that they retain their identity under a soft shell but integrate well with its encompassing CI, and gives to, and take from, benefits, although the soft shell is a double-edged sword in that it is a tool of mild mutual assistance and therefore a cause for envy, prejudice and sometimes persecutions. On the other hand, parasitic CIs cling to a hard shell and are, although willing to take any benefits from, not readily amenable to give any benefits to and are exclusive to the extent of being anti-social. The former and the latter cannot necessarily be clearly demarcated because it is often a result of wider social and historical reactions that they adjust their positions to their best benefits to suit the encompassing demands of their host CI.

Both mitochondrial CIs (M-CI) and parasitic CIs (P-CI) are exclusive to outsiders for religious, racial or whatever reasons. Their difference is a matter of degree and intentions. The former's exclusivity is due to their bonding principles, and otherwise they have no conspiratorial intentions and accommodate, as well as being accommodated by, the wider society, while in the latter's case they tend to have a leverage over and above their bonding principles to stay exclusive, sometimes to the extent of being antisocial (to the host CI). In another word, they use bonding principles to cultivate a group mindset which creates a barrier to defend from, and a weapon to take advantage of, a wider society. $\wedge$ and $\vee$ are both applicable to mitochondrial CIs and parasitic CIs.

A P-CI has an intrinsic tendency to become an M-CI in a $\vee$-encompassing CI because successful (in terms of socio-economic benefits) members realize it is more beneficial to adapt to the wider society and surreptitiously move out of a P-CI. P-CIs, therefore, tend to hollow out in time, and only the fanatical hard core (presumably too dim to adapt to wider communities) stays put. They, thus, become too small to have serious influences in the wider society and decline either to cease or remain eccentric ignorable minor CIs. Any residual reminder of the remaining P-CI becomes an M-CI, more moderate and flexible in their relation with the wider society. Typically I observe this in the Freemasonry CI, which, in the days of more exclusive class-orientated society of 19th century, used to wield substantial power as can be glimpsed in 'War and Peace,' but in our more open and democratically accountable society turned into more of a gentlemen's fraternal club (although occasionally rumours of some misdemeanours can be heard of). On the other hand, in a $\wedge$-encompassing CI any P-CIs are difficult to survive to start with as the most powerful CI in the $\wedge$-model is its inner CI which is really a P-CI in disguise. A P-CI has little reasons to tolerate any other P-CIs. Examples are easy to find, e.g. in the evolution of 17th century Huguenot or 19th century Jewish community in the East End London or factional in-fights especially in the early days of USSR. This is schematically expressed as,

∀ (N › (M › (N→P))) › Λ (N=P), if N ⊦ M and N ⊦ P,

where M is M-CIs, P is P-CIs and N stand for a wider society or nationhood CIs. See the next chapter for the meanings of ›, → and ⊦. It also means that the best way for N to deal with P is not to reject P, but to have an infrastructure readily to suck out successful members of P. On the other hand, in the Λ-model any other P will be stamped out by the only P allowed in that N.

This same expression would pretty much apply to EU (and to the world) if you replaced P-CIs, M-CIs and N respectively with beneficiary nations, benefactor nations and EU. That is, EU's success depends upon its ability and capacity to guarantee any able citizens (and their wealth as well as their wealth creation ability) to move freely and hollow out any nationalistic CIs and incapacitate them. It is usually able men condemned to their perceived inescapable poverty that fan any fanaticisms. The world at large is disturbed by unhappy men who rightly or wrongly perceive their opportunities are unfairly restricted, although room for manoeuvres for changes are currently curtailed by nationhood CIs. EU in this sense is a very unique experiment.

Mentioned above are some of the most significant types of CI, while opposing CIs, overlapping CIs, inclusive CIs are explicit relations of CIs. Active members, passive members are types of members. There may be other types of members and CIs, and also other relations of CIs. However, that is really a matter of demonstrative complexity. Although it may model a certain contemporary situation better, it may just as easily become obsolete. Adhering to the above simplistic model, first of all opposing CIs, overlapping CIs, inclusive CIs are all eventually to be embraced by an all inclusive CI and in the process opposing CIs, and overlapping CIs are dynamically to be transformed into inclusive CIs. The dynamism for this change is innate in the assumption that a whole is more than the sum of parts. That is, parts, be they members or CIs, have an intrinsic tendency to form a whole. A whole can only be inclusive because out of opposing or overlapping parts no cohesive totality can follow. They therefore give rise to the necessity of an encompassing CI which is inclusive by nature.

Examples are found in gender CIs. Male CI and female CI can be seen as opposing or overlapping depending upon various viewpoints, be it sociological, biological or political, etc.. Taken as opposing, shall we say, from a psychological viewpoint, one can encompass them in humanity CI into which they are included as member CIs and a totality is recognized for the benefits of both. Equally, they can be taken as overlapping but exclusive in a small part, say from a socio-economic position as we share more and more equally any burdens of our society, once again an encompassing totality is found, say, in citizenship CI, for the mutual benefits of both, and the small exclusive part (say, motherhood CI) is sanctioned for the benefits of the encompassing CI. Inclusive CIs, on the other hand, are by nature encompassing by themselves.

The process of creating an encompassing CI to rule over opposing CIs and overlapping CIs is accommodated in the assumption that

$$(x) › x,$$

because it is the intrinsic nature of a part to form a whole, and because opposing CIs and overlapping CIs are endowed with this necessity to form a whole. That is, opposing CIs and overlapping CIs necessitate an encompassing CI from within themselves to become a whole. Therefore, › is not just an operator, but an expression of the inner necessity of x. The resultant encompassing CIs are often top-down or mitochondrial because within an encompassing CI legacy parts tend to keep some identity and become inner or mitochondrial CIs. Thus,

$$(x, y, z) › (z, y, x) › (z, (y), x)$$

A mitochondrial CI is by definition a member of an encompassing CI for mutual economical interests. Even when there appears an element of detachment, that is created predominantly for the considerations of economic interests, which have to be mutual in order to be viable. One with unilateral benefits is a parasitical CI, which is, for the purpose of this discourse, not very relevant as it is usually short-lived or very limited in scope of its influence. A parasitical CI is exclusively for the purpose of deriving benefits from a host CI whilst keeping a separate identity. They, therefore, get excluded by excluding. In trying to derive benefits while keeping identity a parasitical CI also tends to radicalize. This is so because exclusion usually works two-ways and, being so, naturally limit benefits which they intend to enjoy. Thus, part of a parasitical CI is inclined to become radically disgruntled. In dealing with any radical elements cohesive magnanimousness is not only the answer, but also the most economic solution. In a cohesive encompassing CI the moderate majority of a parasitical CI gets incorporated via educational and linguistic inclusion and eventually radical elements are either absorbed by the moderate majority or become instead criminal elements like any normal society. The difference between radical elements and criminal elements is the support of moderate majority. The moderate majority, although not joining the radical part for fear of persecution or aggressive reactions, nevertheless, sympathizes with the motives of radicalized colleagues. It is this emotional bond that gives some moral edges to criminal elements and allows them to call themselves victims of radicalization. However, with the moderate majority absorbed into a wider society any radical elements just become criminals and instead of being tragic heroes just follow criminal logic of risks and rewards.

It is intelligence that accommodates overlapping and exclusive CIs because of its ability to create an ever-accommodating CI. All these types and relations of CIs and members play dynamic roles to encourage tangencies and encompassments, eventually leading to Ω. Think of someone giving out leaflets, knocking your door or trying to talk to you, be they political or religious, and why they are doing it. Or, the pleasure of discovering someone speaks your tongue in an unexpected foreign place. Then you know what tangencies and encompassments are at practical levels. It is the necessity of finding a whole out of parts. CIs are empowered to encompass, and it is intelligence that finds a way forward for competing, conflicting and contesting members and CIs. One could say minds are merging to become a whole.

6. Schematized CI
(Logic of Social Modality)

It should be noted that, in order to schematize, it is convenient as well as necessary to idealize the situations concerned so that logical structures can be better distilled. Entities, states of affairs, events, etc. behind concepts and notions used here have many shades, subtleties and exceptions in real life. It would be possible to produce more elaborate versions of schematization by employing complex and flexible concepts and notions, but for a logical purpose it would only make the process of logical extractions unnecessarily time-consuming, although it might produce a more sophisticated narrative presentation. Hopefully, the necessity of simplification did not compromise the logical results obtained. In any events conceptualizations are by necessity idealizations, and readers are free to add their own fresh and bones as they think fit. I only claim a methodological validity.

The basic assumptions are as follows:

Whether the world is finite or infinite, part(s) are always subservient to a whole. Part(s) have an innate necessity to form a whole. This may be more commonly expressed as 'a whole is more than the sum of its parts' as part(s) do not represent this innate necessity by itself as much as the sum of electron, neutron and proton, or of any sub-particles thereof, does not fully explain an atom ontologically or even quantum-mechanically as we know from divergent interpretations of the wave function, although its mathematical total of energy may be conveniently in equilibrium as it is so modelled as it were. Thus,

$(\alpha) \rangle \alpha,$

where α is a part, ( ) is a whole, $\rangle$ is the necessity.

Applying this to a CI, (α) is a CI, while α is a member, › is an operator 'power', meaning α has an intrinsic nature to form (α) and α without ( ) is 'doomed.' Consider an imaginary one-man CI. Whereas a man without self-identity is probably dysfunctional mentally and socially, a man with identity, be it a one-man myth or through a fictitious account of self-creation, has a life, which he tries to maintain and preserve. Such a man, incidentally, is easier to be incorporated into a wider society as it is his identity or desire for identity, whatever it is, that a wider CI finds a purchase for him, or vice versa.

$(\alpha, \beta, \cdots, n)$ › $(\alpha), (\beta), \cdots, (n),$

where n being a countable number optimum to the structure of a CI. Note that $(\alpha, \beta, \cdots, n)$ does not follow from $\alpha, \beta, \cdots, n$ (i.e. $(\alpha, \beta, \cdots, n)$ ‹ $\alpha, \beta, \cdots, n$) because any collections of un-self-identified members do not form any wholes. ‹ is a reverse power to show if $(\alpha, \beta, \cdots, n)$ from $\alpha, \beta, \cdots, n$, then it has an intrinsic nature to collapse back into separate, unidentified $\alpha, \beta, \cdots, n$.

It is a nature of a CI that members are always particular and finite because a CI has a structure that is most efficient at a certain finite number of members. Therefore,

(x) › x

,which is a generalized form of (α) › α, applies to any particulars and concretes of CIs. In general (x) › x applies to any objects of cognitions.

$(\alpha, \beta, \cdots, n, n+1)$ › $(\alpha, \beta, \cdots, n)$

$(\alpha+\beta+ \cdots +n)$ › $(\alpha, \beta, \cdots, n)$

A structure of CI determines the optimum number of members and the strength of their bonding. If the structure of CI is such that allows more members (n+1), then it has more power than one with less numbers (n). '(n+1)' simply means it has more members than '(n)' ('+' is here purely arithmetical). Or, if it allows more cohesive bonding as represented by the operator '+', then it has more power.

There is an optimum number for each CI, where there are structures that allow the arithmetical '+' and the cohesive '+' to combine, like two peaks of synchronizing waves. There are also structures that impose untimely or unsuitable limits on either '+.'

$$(\alpha+\beta+ \cdots +n+(n+1)) \rangle (\alpha, \beta, \cdots, n),$$

where a structure with members both in number and cohesiveness statistically always has more power than one with less numbers and cohesiveness, exceptions being made by unformulable events such as lucks. In between are many deviants, where superiorities between numbers and cohesiveness are not decisive and depend on too many other variables. Therefore,

$$(\alpha+\beta+ \cdots +n+(n+1)) \rangle (\alpha+\beta+ \cdots +n)$$

$$(\alpha, \beta, \cdots, n, (n+1)) \rangle (\alpha, \beta, \cdots, n),$$

where, given similar cohesiveness, or the lack thereof, more numbers usually mean more power, and,

$$(\alpha+\beta+ \cdots +n) \rangle (\alpha, \beta, \cdots, n),$$

where, given similar numbers, more cohesiveness usually means more power. However, as with any statistical statements, 'more' here does not mean 'always' because structures' uniqueness is not always comparable in terms of numbers and cohesiveness.

$$(\alpha+\beta+ \cdots +n) \rangle (\alpha, \beta, \cdots, n, n+1)$$

$$(\alpha, \beta, \cdots, n, (n+1)) \rangle (\alpha+\beta+ \cdots +n),$$

where numbers and cohesiveness are mixed as are the cases in real life, combined with uniqueness of each and every bonding principle, comparisons in terms of 'more power' are more demanding to establish.

The uniqueness of a structure is roughly divided between 'top down' and 'bottom up'. It is always possible to come up with more sophisticated models, but that is simply a matter of demonstrable finesse, which I leave it to someone with more time. Expressing 'top down' as A, 'bottom up' as $\forall$, generally but almost always in a longer term,

$\forall > A$,

because the efficiency of A depends so much on the talents of a few and it is not likely that such talents are always available in a longer time scale. Therefore, although $A > \forall$ is possible at times, the law of statistical averages side with $\forall > A$. The characters of A and $\forall$ are already discussed in some details elsewhere. Thus,

$$\forall (\alpha+\beta+ \cdots +n+(n+1)) > A(\alpha+\beta+ \cdots +n+(n+1)),$$

where a CI which has a structural characteristic of 'bottom up' and attained an optimum number of members with numerical and cohesive superiorities, has a power to domineer over any other CIs. A parametric H is ignored for now as it is yet to appear.

The strength of any bonding principles boils down to its ability to produce benefits for its members. A generally tends to have an inner CI which aims to benefit all members but also benefits from peripheral members of its own CI, and this tendency increases as it degenerates and when it is not easy to deliver benefits from external sources. When this starts to happen, the inner pseudo CI becomes a true CI and A is more and more destabilized. Thus,

$$A(\alpha > \beta > \cdots > n > (n+1)),$$

and this is contradictory and self-destructive because $>$ is only applicable to CIs. When a CI starts to divide into CIs, it has little power to divert externally and either disintegrates or gets encompassed as it loses cohesiveness and numerosity. $\forall$ ideally should not have this problem, although in reality most CIs have shades of both.

Both A and $\forall$ have a vertical structure in order to transmit power internally, which ultimately has to be exerted externally in order to generate uncontaminated benefits to their members. Any internal power that fails to derive benefits externally is contaminated because internal power endorsements generate no overall benefits by themselves. Members agree to the inconvenience of vertical hierarchy so that everyone in the chain is, in the end, rewarded and this reward will not come to the lower ends unless they come from the outside.

This internally transmitted power, therefore, demands an external exit. This is a tangency of a CI and expressed as '→' → entails an encompassment. Thus,

$$CI = \alpha_{\rightarrow}(\alpha),$$

where a minimum CI is defined ('=') as a self-identified individual, which progresses to an optimum CI when a CI contains multiple individuals (members) and power is externalized via a structure. Thus,

$$CI = (\alpha, \beta, \cdots, n) \rightarrow (\alpha), (\beta), \cdots, (n),$$

which could add complexities by incorporating structural characteristics typically such as cohesiveness and numerosity. Structural uniqueness determines those characteristics.

The operator 'power' entails tangencies and encompassments by means of which CIs react with each other. Tangencies are demanded by power and processed according to structural relations between CIs. CIs are related to each other by 'inclusion', 'exclusion' and 'overlap'. Thus, any uniqueness of a CI is externalized by these structural relations between CIs. That is, CIs relate to each other because they are different from each other. Expressing CIs as $p, q, r, \cdots$, etc.,

$$p_{\rightarrow}p(q) , \text{ if only } p \vdash q,$$

where $\vdash$ stands for inclusion and thus p encompasses q and forms an inclusive CI. A CI can only be inclusive because power is an intrinsic nature of a part(s) to form a whole.

$$p_{\rightarrow}p(q_{\rightarrow}q(r)), \text{ if only } p \vdash q \text{ and } q \vdash r,$$

where p encompasses q, which in turn encompasses r and forms an inclusive CI.

In general,

p→p(q→q(r→r(· → · (· → · (N))))), if only p⊦q, q⊦r, r⊦ ·

and · ⊦N,

where N is a CI of a countable number. This represents a general form of an inclusive CI of a countable order and is the most powerful CI, especially if p is ∀-type, +-cohesive and (n+1)-numerative.

p, q, if only p│q (or p‖q, as ‖ is the same as │ for CIs),

where │ and ‖ respectively stand for exclusion and mutual-exclusion and thus p and q are yet unrelated, independent CIs. That is, if p and q exclude each other, they are simply not related. It can never be the case that p includes q, but q excludes p, because a CI is a complete, whole entity, more like a physical object, and therefore although a same member can belong to different CIs, CIs themselves can only relate to each other bilaterally and no part(s) thereof can relate to each other. For the same reason, exclusion and mutual-exclusion do not differ from each other. For a CI, to exclude is of necessity to be excluded. Members can, and often does, belong to CIs that conflict with each other because they are only concerned with net overall benefits to themselves and are psychologically and intellectually complex enough to handle various opposing elements of facts of life within each accommodating capacities. It is not wise or safe to entrust oneself to one single CI and we often play double, triple games so as to diversify risks. A CI itself, however, cannot play such games because it only behaves as a totality. CIs can only encompass or be encompassed. Exclusive CIs will eventually find a tangency and any failure to encompass or be encompassed will result in the loss of their identity.

p→(p(q), p(r)), even if q│r when x│q and x│r,

where q and r are held together in the inclusive p for the temporary benefits of protection from x (not meant to be a free variable) which is exclusive from both q and r. This will disintegrate as soon as x is removed and therefore p no longer generates any benefits, thus by being encompassed or by encompassing.

q, r if only q | r, or

$x \rightarrow x(p)$,

where q and r are again unrelated, independent CIs or encompassed by x.

$p \rightarrow p(q, r)$, when q ‖ r,

where ‖ stands for overlap (‖ is of necessity bilateral for the same reason as | and ‖ and therefore q ‖ r is also r ‖ q, because for a CI, to overlap is the same as being overlapped) and p is a pseudo inclusive CI that contains both q and r. However, p that exists between q and r, either predominates the overall relation between q and r or q and r will eventually exclude each other, because a CI is only inclusively divisible. Neither q nor r can have a separate identity within itself which generates benefits only for a part of q or r. In that case q and r would break up.

Any complexities that arise from exclusion, overlap and number of CIs, etc., and any combinations thereof, are dynamically removed by tangencies and encompassments of inclusive CIs, which eventually converge into Ω.

$(p \rightarrow p(q \rightarrow q(r \rightarrow r(\cdot \rightarrow \cdot (\cdot \rightarrow \cdot (N)))))) \rightarrow \Omega$,

where Ω signifies less and less CIs in the process of encompassments and ends in the final inclusive CI in vacuum. This is an inevitable function of → when N can only be a countable finite number because with nothing to encompass there will be no tangencies.

The internal power within $p \rightarrow p(q \rightarrow q(r \rightarrow r(\cdot \rightarrow \cdot (\cdot \rightarrow \cdot (N)))))$ that generates benefits must then transcend into an entity that can sustain without creating benefits. This is a tangency to encompass itself and transform itself into an extra-socioeconomic entity. Thus,

$CI = (p \rightarrow p(q \rightarrow q(r \rightarrow r(\cdot \rightarrow \cdot (\cdot \rightarrow \cdot (N)))))) \rightarrow \Omega$

is the form of history and is embodiable extra-temporarily when N is sufficiently small. This may be called a personal enlightenment and is where life in space can meet life in time. Ω is a CI in vacuum, which contends with non-material benefits, which can only be intellectual since I regard so-called spiritual or religious benefits as fictional.

In the process towards Ω we overcome nationhood CIs, which, although they appear so domineering, have been in steady decline ever since their peak in 19th century. I did mention catastrophes as a catalyst, but there are many historical movements at work that seem to be accelerating this process.

The heightening awareness of human rights is becoming a universal constant to restrain the internal power transmissions of nationhood CIs and to limit their tangencies. More generally this is a constant that is restrictive over vertical structures and exaggerative over horizontal structures and is also a relationship catalyst. Thus, expressing human rights as h,

$$A / h^2 = \forall / h,$$

where h is a constant as every CI must conform to them, and h^2 in order to reflect the dual CI structure of A and prevailing subdued state of human rights inherent in A. Be it a top-down CI or a bottom-up CI, they are both equally constrained by human rights. The former may be more resilient to start with, but the fall will come dramatically (see recent events in North Africa), while the latter will be forced to transform surreptitiously but steadily through legal adaptations (see how the society was forced to embrace gay marriages, female bishops, minority rights, etc.., etc..)

Although h may look a recent arrival, it was always there in various shapes of natural sentiments; sympathies towards life, empathies for fellow human beings, benevolent/religious charities, etc.., across cultures and geographies. It was the relative socioeconomic enrichments of the poor through political rights, social welfares and tax systems combined with the fall of the so-called elite males through their own misdemeanours, stupidity and greed that brought the so-called underclass to the position of collective influence, currently through the new media. Monetarily it is also the decline of absolute power of money (the less monetized world), and also the society is more difficult to govern, considering money is the most important tool of governance (the rise of horizontal forces against the vertical power structures). Horizontal forces are yet to invent a currency of governance, other than their ability to produce celebrities. h will eventually create a parametric H.

This less monetized world took the wars of 20th century to achieve and is built on a floor for social deprivations as a recompense for general mobilizations; such is the price of arming the innocent underclass for the errors of privileged elite males. For those who hear the outcries of unequal distributions of wealth today, just think of the brutal power of money in the Dickensian world, which was historically not long ago and in the mightiest and wealthiest empire. It is the floor, not the ceiling, that proves the more benevolent nature of our worlds. Today's homeless people always have something to wear, usually something in the stomach and basic care often provided by society, while in the Dickensian world there was certain actual starvation, selling of daughters and abundant fallen women. Think about debtors' prisons and Jack the Ripper's prostitutes. For a man with money and weak moral like the latter-day Uriah Heap the world must have looked like walking oysters.

This floor of deprivations can be renamed 'human rights,' which set horizontal brakes to the vertical power mechanism of CIs. All these do not tell how we advanced in such a short space and time, or such advancement was necessarily due, but rather show fundamentally abysmal nature of our characters. Given any relapses, we will be back to square one in no time. The notion of human rights without religious or ideological connotations is not only the greatest socio-economic invention of 20th century but also of human history. This will need most careful nurturing and conscious guarding and administrations. Otherwise, it could surreptitiously end up assimilated and incorporated into a tool of vertical power.

Likewise, the rising power awareness of females will at some stage force nationhood CIs to review their status quo internally and externally, especially in Islamic circles. The appearance of horizontal forces because of the advent of new media will challenge the vertical power bases of nationhood CIs in more widespread manners, once their spontaneity is augmented by sustainability.

In addition, post-singularity artificial intelligence will know no national boundaries and challenge human intelligence, or the lack thereof, in its wisdom to liaise with nationhood CIs.

All in all, nationhood CIs are doomed in their current forms and are well advised to be Ω-aware in their various attempts for survival. I do not know what the immediate next stage from nationhood CIs is but Ω-compatible transformations will help less turbid historical changes.

Ω is a stage where we all share a same identity and seek growth not in generating more and more socio-economic benefits but in intellectual satisfactions. Ω is a stage where we will be more severely tested and reveal whether we are just over-extended animals or something that manifests the meaning of life instead of being bearers of life. With Ω, we qualify to represent 'Earth Logic,' which is the most abstract form of life borne and cultivated by our planet and condenses all our intellectual achievements. We seek satisfactions in finding, refining and preserving 'Earth Logic.' Incidentally post-singularity artificial intelligence is something magically near Ω and may leapfrog every human endeavour to reach Ω.

7. Topical Approaches

7.1. As Things Stand

As things stand today, from historical perspectives we live in an era of unprecedented plenty and peace. When one hears about the death of dozens in a blast in Syria or elsewhere or a starving woman's cry in Congo or elsewhere, historically speaking, it is not a sign of misery and despair but rather a symbol of how far we came from the days when such matters were not even worth talking about. Even a few decades before, without counting two world wars, a death of thousands did not easily become world news. There were many little massacres here and there, which we were not even remotely aware of. Demands for foods were not a matter of human rights but a privilege for a lucky few.

In this context, the notion of CIs looks irrelevant. In fact, many people have layers of CIs consciously or unconsciously and often depending upon convenience, and sometimes even opposing CIs. With or without the notion of CIs to complicate our view of the world, the conventional market economy seems functioning reasonably despite many so-called crises. However, CIs become important when resources become limited and one need to enhance whatever benefits one can get hold of. In general, tightly held group structures are more prevalent where livings are tougher. It is our temporary state of luxury that we can afford to ignore CIs. I would call this ionization of CIs into charged individuals. It appears as if individuals are so empowered that they are capable of living by themselves. This misconceived state is today called democracy.

Just as the nationhood CIs took foothold in the void of loosening religious CIs and in the wake of industrialization coupled with the loss of the grip of the landed aristocracy, charged individuals are only waiting a new structure that create more benefits than the nationhood CIs. This will happen where the nationhood CIs fail to embrace new information tools for the benefits of individuals and instead use them in order to exert more control over individuals. We are so to speak in the state of plasma caused by the loss of faith in the nationhood CIs, and democracy is a name not for empowered individuals but for waning nationhood powers.

It was the industrial revolution that had the biggest impact on human history and gave rise to an impetus to nationhood CIs. We are having the second revolution (IT revolution), which is, with the coming of new mindsets, yet to have a more fundamental impact and replace nationhood CIs with something less vertical or transform them into more horizontal structures as readily available information makes the society more transparent, accountable and even.

Our time of plenty (of foods, entertainments and information) appears disguised in the name of human rights. This prompts the dilution of the nationhood CI and the proliferation of trans-border CIs. Although one would imagine that given long overdue catastrophes the centralization of CIs may give rise to the recall of the nationhood CI, this newly acquired rights will prevent the reemergence of the nationhood CI. As the nationhood CI was itself a product of time and place, we should not miss too much about its dilution.

Individuals are not capable of producing any benefits by themselves. It is via interactions with other individuals and groups of individuals that benefit them and more so for some individuals depending upon where one stands in power structures. It is in the misconceived name of democracy that we take it for granted that we should all be fed, clothed, and roofed. Thus, it is when the conventional 'democratic' social structure fails to deliver what is taken for granted that individuals would be reminded of the fictitious nature of so-called human rights and that without appropriate CIs to define and guarantee there are no human rights by natural law.

What awaits us is the collapse of this false security of human rights as if enshrined by divine interventions. It only takes a few famines we will start ignoring so-called human rights as it is always a priority that we feed ourselves first. No individuals have human rights unless they belong to some CI which co-exists with other CIs in agreement to cherish the rights of individuals for the sake of ensuring the survival of CIs themselves.

Mono-cultural nations, like some of Far Eastern nations, may be enjoying a good fortune of stability, being relatively free from waves of immigrations, illegal or otherwise, or terrorism, but will be left behind as they fail to assimilate the necessity of history toward an ever-encompassing whole. That is, being mono-cultural may be a short-term asset and long-term liability in an inevitably smaller and smaller world, unless the notion of a national culture as a politico, socio-economic asset thins out so much that it bears little significance. Japan may be heading that way, being essentially non-religious and culturally blind as it is literally a cultural island of its own facing little alien competitions from any other cultures, even fully embracing so-called 'Americanization.' A cultural virgin like a penguin brought up without fears of enemies with more curiosity than with alertness for predators, so to speak, although all too easily, it may wake up to be a world-wary madam if abashed with too much unwanted attention.

The multi-cultural nations like US and UK, although occasionally appear precarious, are actually more in tune with the historical destiny. Even the whistleblower of the internet espionage does a credit to the encompassing ability of US if a card is played right, as it could only happen to US. Should a similar eventuality occur in China or Russia, the likely outcome would have been more silent and deadly. Many nations including Japan and UK surreptitiously and indulgently wish to make use of US-CI when convenient in the name of special relationship if only to fend off the potentially exclusive CIs like China and Russia.

However, there is obvious loss of libido for US-CI, not unlike the end of the Roman Empire. One might call it a structural fatigue. In essence it is a CI that extended beyond their structural optimum capacities and lost its vigor by failing to innovate itself to cope with an environment it helped to create. Much of its strength appears to have been sucked away by emerging powers, ironically not so much by their merits but more by its own greed and stupidity, or by its failure to appreciate the nature of its own nationhood CI. Much as the fall of Roman Empire can be attributed to the systemic failure of plunder-based economy more and more relying on the use of mercenaries, any democratic system based on market economy heavily investing in a non-democratic one party system is self-contradictory and is akin to spitting to the sky. Here, economic needs are failing to see to political necessities, allowing short-term gains to create their own long-term demise. Although they may think they are playing for time (hoping the opponent will be transformed to be one of them), it is more likely they are playing into the hands of the opponent, because a paradigm shift of A to $\forall$ requires $A / h^2 = \forall / h$, while h^2 literally risks the collapse of a A-CI. The inner CI of a A-CI will not trade its benefits for the human rights of its outer CI.

Add on top of this the like of preaching human rights while breaching them (tortures, extraordinary renditions, evades-droppings on fellow world leaders, etc..), or being by far the worst per capita polluter of environments while ingratiating itself to the rest of world for containing the worst gross polluter into slowing down, you get a picture of a bishop fornicating with the wife of an archdeacon. From a CI's point of view, whatever US get out of these misdemeanors it is hardly worth to the damages to its brand. If their politicians are incapable of appreciating such simple facts, then one wonders if they are signs of structural malaises.

Events-driven politics of the democratic West have no politicians of any caliber, and situations are moving around like on the Ouija board. Events are formed by unseen collective fingers of mediocrity and greed initiated in Middle East and Russia. China is poised to take advantages of any unintended consequences without accosting itself, with its population crazed with money under the faked ideology of communism, which destroyed the elegance of their ceramics, poetry and paintings their ancestors created but failed to replace with any noteworthy noble crafts or arts.

In the limelight of myriads and multitudes of the social media, everyone becomes actors and actresses, a little not unlike the world of politics. Mr. Nobody is suddenly a hero or villain to leave his name in history, just think of a few names relating 9/11 or Arab Spring. So-called extremists or radicals are very much in this category. In the psychology of petty mediocrity one finds answers to the flourishing industry of radicals, be they terrorists or religious fanatics. This is a way for someone with little real talents or abilities to become an instant public figure with more than willing helps even from the traditional media. Religions play an easiest and cheapest cover for excuses and give legitimate fronts to a simple soul who wants to play a soldier for a fun to start with, without thinking too much about consequences for himself and others. Religions are modus operandi of pseudo-political gangster organizations while monies are their modus vivendi. Look no farther than good, old Japanese Yakuza.

All these are not really a problem if the limelight comes and goes to give temporary amusements to a stage of fools once in a while. However, the new social media gives it a totally new perspective. The limelight is on permanently, encouraging everyone to try to become an actor or actress. Thus, it is the social media that is encouraging radicals, like a nameless little girl called Sadie with her little brother suddenly becoming a world celebrity for a day or two, although I must admit I was philosophically entertained by her (and am now worried for her should she develops into a parrot). The problems with actors and actresses are that they tend to act, and always on the side of exaggerations. Thus, we now have a culture of exaggerations, and radicals will not go away. Three things will change this. The limelight should be controlled (like China or Russia), the fates of actors and actresses should be encouraged to played through to tragic ends, or await the emergence of new mindsets with more immunity to these instant celebrities. It will come as the varied combinations of all three, but the last is the only real solution.

In our time of the culture of exaggerations and role plays, one could easily wander into the corridors of terrorists and jihadists, not dissimilar to mere 16-year-old boys and unemployed youths being enticed into the ways of the army life through propagandas. They are more fascinated by guns rather than any ideologies behind. In either way lacks of prospects, information and education as well as misguided perceptions of our society and history bring them into the sordid ways of violence, be it recognized institutions or murderous adventure holidays under the faked banners of religions. There is room for psychologists, or even psychiatrists here. Considering only a superficial difference at the level of foot soldiers (remember (prince) Harry in SS uniform), the former will, in fact, make a good latter after removing religious pretences. Social engineering is the key. Swap the pleasure of cheap Kalashnikovs and brutal hard works without overtime pays with a medal, pension and hope, glory and gratifications of a grateful nation. Not too difficult a task for a psychologist who can bring up their children into anything. It should be noted that some ill-reputed politicians, like Blair, who conjures up such an ugly image of themselves in sharp contrast to Thatcher's dignified post-PM posture, speaking up against this and that, have precisely opposite effects. Politicians in general who lost credibility and public trusts do not have much effect in anything they say. In terrorists' role plays there is an element of angry young disillusioned individuals fighting against less credible nationhood CIs, although, like Arab Spring, removing nationhood CIs without preparing for the next stage only brings miseries and disruptions of worst kind and in fact prolongs the life of failing nationhood CIs.

In these days of media proliferations, politicians too play games of exaggerations, especially of exaggerated fears (remember Blair/Bush speeches on Saddam's weapons of mass destruction), speaking up for the sake of it, giving unnecessary twists to uncomplicated and benign situations to have their celebratory role plays. In the same veins, radicals are made even more radical, extremists are turned into monsters, and they too are forced to play their fanatic roles by expectations and exaggerations, as actors and actresses. The social media is turning our plain life into stage plays. The society should find a way of immunity via CIs where irrelevant celebrities do not have undue places to influence the natural evolution of CIs. Such mindsets will hopefully grow out of the society tired of cheap celebrities, stage-play politicians, actor terrorists and easy label religions. Or, are we such hopeless and tireless gossip-mangers that the world has to be pushed around by our inner ghoulish journalists who feed on schadenfreudean needs of newsworthy miseries? We will find out by having even more of exaggerations for now. It is still early days of the social media.

Events driven politics of today also mean politicians act like house-keepers, tending and mending here and there. Ideas and ideologies are frowned upon as they generally proved not only wrong, but also dangerous and useless. So we all settled on the petty world of market economy, where everyone is busy attending their affairs of more profits, less taxes and greater worldly enjoyments. Democracy descends into 'mediocracy' ('mobocracy' for less institutionalized countries (remember Arab Spring) or 'quangocracy' for well-regulated nations) of wanting something for nothing and caters for the needs of the lowest common denominators. Politicians are there to ensure happiness is concocted out of the blend of greed and consumptions. Those who missed out on this worldly boat of happiness protest under the faked banners of religions and seek schadenfreudean joys by inflicting miseries on those even less fortunate as they can neither reach or understand the source of their unhappiness.

Politicians, with their absolutely disproportional influences over the population, are the only vocation and profession (and it is becoming more and more so) which does not officially require any qualifications, while doctors or lawyers have to go through rigorous trainings and tests to be on an appropriate register to practice. All they are required is a talent for cleaver talks, a quick mind to win debates and appeasing manners, and above all, a skill to say what the mass want to hear and not even to murmur what they really think, as well as being sons, grand sons and kin of (some-times disgraced) PMs and presidents. Remember it was the same president who could not spell that staged an illegal war for a mis-placed revenge, which was, when turned out to be groundless, conveniently emphasized for a necessity for democracy, which remains unresolved to this day in the midst of corruptions and ter-rorisms, and also whereas that necessity could be found virtually anywhere. Remember also that if an ability to win a debate is a po-litical asset, then politics is becoming a show game, which no wonder gives leverage to horizontal forces, with the result that it is getting more and more difficult to win a clear mandate to govern.

It is a high time now, after so many mediocrities not fit to lead and the trend of politics becoming family businesses, that they were required to have some basic understandings and skills in or-der to regain respectability and cultivate intellect to formulate genuine policies to lead. I propose that a PhD in history and pref-erably as well as in economics, are mandatory to becoming profes-sional politicians, still easier than becoming medical consultants. Then, we may have more respectable political scenes across the globe. Alternatively, party politics will be swept aside by waves of horizontal forces as coalitions become the norm of politics and the directionless current of weak politicians mingled with corrupt des-pots will form a period of history, governed by the will (and greed) of the populace which tantamount to the petty minded concerns for their own pockets. There may even be a party that advocate internet direct democracy if we can trust people. But, then since it is people who have to take consequences of any political failures, I see why not.

There are signs of the death-throe of nationhood CIs. Ideas and ideologies do not work because they tend to stem from, and are based upon, nationhood CIs. If you realize it is nationhood CIs themselves that are coming to the end of a useful life, then you also realize you should seek alternatives to these CIs which served us some 250 years neither rightly nor wrongly, but as the historical process demanded. Our new environments of the social media and entangled mass of humanity will spew out an alternative and higher CI. How to institutionalize this new CI and give it a legal status is a task we should start engaging in.

Currently we participate in politics through nationhood CIs. A general loss of interest in politics as we observe coincides with the loss of the vigour of nationhood CIs. We anticipate something higher and larger than nationhood CIs, although we cannot quite point our finger at it. However, generally it would be in the direction of more organized and stronger horizontal forces expressed through entrenched human rights, the new media, gender equalization and intelligent voting. One might call it the internet democracy or the digital power. After all, if the Inland Revenue is happy to pursue monies, which are the oxygen of our very society, via the on-line tax return, even that will be soon replaced by intelligent data collection, I fail to see why the direct democracy cannot be achieved through the same media. The archaic parliamentarian proxy democracy, which lost respects and trusts of the society, should be replaced with the new internet direct democracy and better qualified IT administrators. The next stage from nationhood CIs is unthinkable without internet and artificial intelligence.

7.2. Economy

Finally for those individuals who prefer to spend a life as comfortably as possible, here is a good advice. Do not participate in any CIs, other than the self-identifying CI, which you need in order to know what it is you want. Ignore any so-called modern conveniences and learn to live frugally and modestly, ideally with minimum physical needs. Acquire a way of being a non-social as against being an anti-social. For any extra benefits you may enjoy as member of a CI, even of an inner CI, you tend to overexert yourself for those who benefit even more, who are cleverer, more determined and skilful in manipulating their colleagues. In the end, you will know you lived for those others and least for yourself. The three most costly things in your life will be car, wife and house, and if you can dispense with one or two of these your life will improve dramatically in terms of a stress level.

For those ordinary morsels who cannot help becoming members of CIs for physical as well as psychological needs consciously or unconsciously, or those who enjoy proactively being members of CIs in search of self, petty as it may be, the next best thing is to ride a CI without being involved. You are Machiavellians, although a Machiavellian in Machiavelli's sense is slightly more noble-minded. This way you get what you pay. You exert yourself for the benefits you expect. This is playing a game and you can play better if you are not emotionally involved. Those who are at inner CIs or at the top layers of membership are often non-believers. They are flexible and accommodate multiple CIs at will. They are in a sense a free member of CI. Economy is often driven by those members of convenience, who are there for himself. Economy driven by the self-interest of the rich is self-destructive in so far as it cannot keep deriving benefits from its own members to please its own members. Aggressive market economy owes its present to its future as it equates the present credit with the future debt. A so-called democratic political structure led by mediocre politicians also manages the present at the expense of the future. They are mediocre because giving is always easier than taking; especially when they are more concerned with being elected.

Much as power is not exercisable if evenly distributed, money is less absolute if possessed equally. Within democracy are institutions of governance that have to be powered. Likewise, economy functions on money, which, markets, by definition, distribute diversely. Democracy is a word that contains many contradictions. Allowing democracy since most alternatives are even less desirable or trustworthy, CIs are the bringer of solution to these contradictions. However, at Ω democracy is attained at the expense of economy since markets become dysfunctional among fellow members. In a situation where no one wins over anyone, competitions cease and contentions avail. For us not to be bored with such a peace we will have to be intelligent as well as intellectual. Here, $\Omega \rangle \sim\Omega$ bears a question mark.

Likewise, the value of money is relative and not absolute. Money is worth because it is unevenly distributed. Power is only exercisable if it lacks uniformity. An organization is dysfunctional without hierarchical structure, like a military with a same rank for all. Even the functionality will have to be translated into some sort of hierarchical structure. This is the meaning of power. Greenspanean market economy's spectacular fall into disgrace was only rescued at the expense of market itself. In monetizing debts central banks exceeded their remits of trust, revealing their inability to apprehend markets, let alone to control them. They thought they could manipulate markets as Greenspan did. Markets do only what markets are supposed to do. That is to respond to environments through price mechanisms. Monetized debts equate to the denial of price mechanisms and ultimately money itself. Central banks are there to guard the value of money and are entrusted with the welfare of society present and future.

Although they did only what they could do at the time of this crisis. Nevertheless, what has been done is the acknowledgement of the failure of their missions and functions. Like 'numbers' money is simply 'units' assigned to power for the running of society, not itself receptacles of power even in desperation. Forcing the middle class and future generations to pay for the failure of central bankers and their political counterparts, even for the protection of the poor, whose job is inevitably to pretend to be even poorer (and incidentally the further enrichment of the rich), money has changed its meaning. I shall term this as the law of squeezed middle; any governments so stupidly indebted as to need resorting to printing money cannot get out of the trouble without squeezing the middle unless they deliberately intend to inflate their way out, while unwittingly enriching the rich and driving the poor poorer (relative to the rich, not to the middle). Incidentally, many politicians and central bankers belong to the rich. It has become a political tool embedded with power of necessity, nonetheless of arbitrariness. Like numbers embedded with objects, instead of being 'units,' money has now become more powerful, but with more limited usages, together with a consequence of failure. Monetized debts based society is a society made governable more than ever by relying on the paradigm of vertical mechanisms and goes against the historical process towards less vertical and more horizontal society, unless, of course, it is destined to fail and bring forward a horizontal structure unexpectedly early.

The crisis may be abating like calm before a storm. There is a price yet to pay. As with nationhood CIs, this historical crisis is telling us not to shelve but to face it, if not through inflation as theoretically envisaged but as yet failed to materialize, through a new paradigm of economy as will be forced by being politicized. It is signalling the end of greed and consumption based so-called market economy that defined us post WW II to the end of 20th century. Money used to be credits to purchase goods and services, plain and simple. It has now acquired a life of its own through monetized debts and politically motivated negative real interest rates engineered to reflate economy. Politicians proudly used to say they gave independence to their central bank, whereas it was central bankers who became politicians and politicians have to dance to the tunes of central bankers' music. No wonder some central bankers have to get paid 10 times as much as a Prime Minister. Instead of products of economic activities, it is economic activities that are products of this new politicized money. Instead of being master of money, we are now addicts and slaves of this opiate money. This could turn out to be the harbinger of a catastrophe to nail the fate to nationhood CIs. This opiate money may kill pains, but does not cure or heal. Meanwhile we are so addicted that we forget what these pains are trying to tell; the economic model based on consumptions, wastes and greed has come to its useful limits. From the lack of imaginations and the fear of backlashes from disgruntled voters not only are we desperately trying to reflate this old model, but also to propagate it to emerging worlds by default (Quantitative Easing [QE] ripple-effects) and in the hope that it will be generations 50 years hence who pay our price.

Monetized debts, without which most of the world's largest economies would have experienced materially serious negative impacts on the fortunes of their nationhood CIs and, therefore, by implications, of practically all other nationhood CIs as well as other CIs, such as corporate CIs and community CIs. It can also be said the emergence of such as Brics and other EM nationhood CIs owes greatly to the monetized debts of major economies. They all significantly contributed to the worsening environments and some of them even come to pose the threat of instability to the world (butterfly effects of monetization). The outcome of monetization, although giving us some respite, is yet by no means certain and could indeed end all of us in tears.

It should be noted that Quantitative Easing (QE) is the denial of the market mechanism on which our market economy (and hence the so-called current Western socio-economic model) is based, to pay for political failures at the expense of the middle class wealth. Furthermore, no politicians, central bankers were made accountable for their grave errors. One could even say that it is the biggest insider dealing because governments are funding themselves by issuing debts, which should be seen intrinsically riskier, at a price they directly manipulate and takes no account of any risk premiums. The situation is not dissimilar to a family living off by handing out IOUs instead of working harder. We are on borrowed time before actually going bankrupt, but the problem is that we are all part of that family, and there seem to be no alternatives because we are all mired in this failed economic model. QE distorts the financial market from corner to corner, by products as well as by geography. Anything with price on, equity, fixed income, commodities, property, etc.., are grotesquely over- or under-priced by printed money. The end-game is far from over. This distortion is only allowed on the assumption the market resumes its normal functions before it is hit by another tidal waves, which seem a distinct possibility as the contagion is now spreading to EM, where QE is not possible without hyperinflation.

Our model served us well for the economy of necessary and even of indulgence. The current difficulties which we are desperately trying to get over by monetization, and the forced diminution of the middle class wealth is that faced with the economy of unnecessary our model based on greed and consumptions no longer works and need to be replaced with something more intellectual that can translate the need for perpetual growth into sustainable value creation. The efforts to spur growth through monetized debts and forced diminutions of the middle class wealth will barely give us time to seek alternatives, and we are steadily failing to do so. The economic uncertainty will create hazards to nationhood CIs. Instead of smooth transitions to some higher CIs nationhood CIs will desperately try to hang on, seek undesirable solutions and blame everything else but themselves. As always, it is mediocre politicians' fate to wait until too late, and to tread symptomatically. Various undesirable events such as terrorism, religious fanaticism, failed states, dilution of sovereignty, etc.., are symptoms of failing nationhood CIs. Politicians, economists, sociologists, historians, etc.., must act together now to seek alternative models of economy as well as of nationhood CIs.

It would be too good to be true if we can get over this crisis of centuries by printing money. Politicians are too complacent and untrustworthy to rely on for the true aftermaths of this crisis. They are too focused on election cycles and, be they politicians, bankers or even academics, they all have enough, if not too much, savings to tide over and hide away in case of any unpleasantries. The answer must come from the long-suffering and easy-to-target middle class, who nobody bothers asking any opinions for alternatives to the current economic models and nationhood CIs. They are the ones who took and have yet to take any consequences. From the tsunami of the social media new CIs will emerge to take over the next stage of encompassments. The expected self-corrections of our democratic politico-economic model a la Chicago School are not forthcoming because the next stage of CIs is not an evolution within the $\forall$- paradigm, but rather a paradigm shift from $\forall$-model to a new horizontalized CI, H.

There are serious social changes that have impacts on the shape of economy: A family CI is formed by biological benefits and sustained by socio-economic benefits which are internal as per any group structures as well as external imposed by a larger encompassing CI. These external benefits arise because the so-called society, which is composed of many specific inclusive or overlapping CIs such as corporate CIs, religious CIs, community CIs, etc.., work in tandem to encourage family CIs to maintain the status-quo by means of socio-economic benefits given in the forms of e.g. allowances, taxes, social recognitions and encouragements, stigma, etc.. This is changing consciously or unconsciously because a family CI based on the implicitly inferior position of a female is becoming less viable and tenable as the society at large concedes to feminist demands on equal status in every socio-economic sphere. The dwindling external benefits on family CIs bring about changes in the status of family CIs, including reductions of family CIs (and of children by implication, at least of happy children as we used to know) as males no longer see benefits in forming such CIs and females have less incentive to sustain such CIs at the expense of even pretending an inferior position, once biological benefits are attained. This is one of biggest upheavals in human history and forces changes and adjustments in virtually everything in socio-economic mechanisms. The sooner one adapt to this new realism as individuals and CIs, the more successful in tangencies and encompassments. That is, any higher encompassing CIs are ones which adapted to this change. The implications of the gender equalization also have a much wider scope than family benefits. Socio-economic impacts of male-female relationship behavioural changes will be felt through consumptions patterns and volumes.

7.3. Human Rights

At a time when we are keenly made aware that our natural resources are running out, human population seem to have an uncontrollable upward momentum and, believe or not, we are enjoying a historically unprecedented peace time coupled with highly consumption-based economy, the human rights issue seems almost counter-intuitive and overtly pandering. As a matter of demand and supply if any, human rights should decrease in value. This contradictory phenomenon is due to the emergence of a new CI that will eventually replace nationhood CIs, which currently seem to predominate over our life. Nationhood CIs themselves are going through character transformations, which eventually lead to a paradigm shift.

From the days of ruthless imperial ambitions and exploitations to the two world wars nationhood CIs experienced the crises of their *raison d'être*, first for some, as straightforward victims, then as it dawned on us that none of us could be winners. That is, it is not possible to pursue the self-interest of a nation regardless of its neighbors. Even so-called market economy does not really allow truly free competitions, restricted by currencies, taxations, regulations and above all political considerations. At the same time, nationhood CIs still have an impetus because socio-economic systems and their institutions are designed around the paradigm of nationhood CIs, and because we are not yet clear what we want replace nationhood CIs with. It is this impending feeling that nationhood CIs are metamorphosing into something new that is named 'human rights.'

When a starving villager in a remote corner of darkest Africa cries out human rights to be fed and cared for, she is not pointing out the shortcomings of her own country, nor is she appealing to our moral obligations, she is suggesting she belongs to the humanity CI which transcends nationhood CIs and we are ignoring her pleas at our own perils because her plights today could be our plights tomorrow in our days of very small world where everything is interconnected. In short, she is reminding us she is also covered by the 'insurance' under the humanity CI, which is not yet institutionalized but now has come to exist as more than just desires.

Remember that a holy idiot like the one in Karamazov was cared for not out of any deliberate Christian compassion but as a norm of village life, no matter how poor it is. This unconscious act of humanity is observed across religions and cultures and is based on the feelings that given circumstances, we are all same. It is possible this village idiot is related to many in the village considering how communities used to be isolated (until recently people used to stay within the range of tens of miles for hundreds and thousands of years from recent DNA studies in UK), and we are all biologically related anyway, descended from the seven daughters of Eve or the like, going back to the original mitochondrial mother figure. It is just that an idiot in a Russian village was replaced by one in a global village.

The issue of human rights is, therefore, an inevitable consequence of our socio-economic developments, and the model of a nationhood CI has become outdated and outmoded. In my schematic presentation of history human rights would become a constant of relational catalyst which is restrictive over nationhood CIs, corporate CIs, etc.., i.e. over vertical power structures, and exaggerative over horizontal forces. Thus, the human rights constant is positively applicable to horizontal forces and negatively operative on vertical powers, unless CI-progressions are catastrophe-based transformations. This constant will metamorphose into a parametric Һ, once horizontal forces consolidate into a sustainable structure and start to transmute nationhood CIs into a higher encompassing CI.

E.g. such as the appearance of celebrities and the spectacular rise of popular sports, which allow people of often below ordinary intellectual capacities and educational achievements to speak up in the matters of national importance and even influence pandering politicians, are one of the direct results of the new media and the emergence of a CI larger than nationhood CIs. So-called elite males who have run the affairs of state over centuries proved just as stupid and incompetent in providing securities and prosperities as can be observed in war after war at the expense of what they call plebs. Dare I mention the likes of Bush-Blair who could little foresee even darker shadows in the shades of Saddam Hussein, whose superficial demise they choreographed together, but in his death (if it was worth dying for) it was Saddam who ridiculed and outsmarted them both with his street wisdom by tainting the two self-proclaimed world leaders, not to mention thousands of US-UK military lives and billions of tax payers' money and the ever bigger aftermath mayhems. No wonder footballers, chefs and actresses are little worse to comment on the running of governments. At least, they do less damage.

'Human rights,' which seem to act as a brake over war-mongering nationhood CIs, are a seal of the incompetence of the self-important men of governance and an acknowledgement of the superiority of the commonsense of ordinary men and women. A humanity CI is, thus, a horizontal power as against vertical powers that run our history so far and is a precursor to a supra-national, borderless network CI supported by wider humanity replacing staatsräson.

When I say the world is more horizontal, some simplistic economists (I even seem to recall some recent Nobel Prize winner) might rightly or wrongly, depending upon statistical methodologies and validity of data, say the distribution of wealth is more polarized. Here, one should distinguish between the essential wealth and the imaginary wealth. The former is for basic necessities, the latter is for so-called luxuries and is catered for by the price mechanism of our consumption-based market economy. The distinction is between a function and a social fiction, of a good. One only need to realize a £50k cottage in rural Scotland can meet the entire basic needs of a roof over one's head as much as a £200m mansion in Knightsbridge, or nearer to home, a £3 bottle of cider, as good as a £400 bottle of vintage Krug. The difference is in perceptions. Having more of the latter does not really equate having thousand times more wealth. You only imagine it because you are deluded by fictional prices. In terms of the essential wealth, we are generally much more equal than any other times in history because of the enhanced social welfares, better and wider public services and more socialist taxation systems as well as variously improved political rights.

It is human rights embraced through these socio-economico-political infrastructures, and even charities, that today provide a considerable portion of the essential wealth. It is in these aspects that we live in a more horizontal world and do not have to bow to someone simply because he has more money, whereas not long ago a small difference in fortune made the difference of freedom or debtor's prison, or of lady or tart. To think of the possession of goods priced £1m (come to think of it, not much nowadays, say a small flat in Chelsea or a few Ferraries) is a wealth worth any respect is rather lack of intelligence. As a biological entity there is a limit one needs or can consume or waste in terms of physical materials, the rest is a fiction of the price mechanism. Consume a 1 kg of best Beluga caviar at £2,000 everyday, not only you get tired of after 3 days, if not 1 day, but also more likely you will be dead after 6 months. Take away any essential wealth, that means more vertical worlds, where power is skewed upwards and what should have been imaginary wealth start taking on essential colours. Even the economic wealth cannot just be measured in monetary terms. In order to be used, any wealth has to be eventually translated into goods and services. Most of the imaginary wealth will be fictionally priced. That is why a van Gogh painting which had no monetary value in his life time comes to be valued at, say, $100m. Putting both types of wealth in a same basket and arguing how unequal our world has become, is the same as mixing oil and water. The evolution of human rights should be viewed as the distribution of the essential wealth. A rich man cannot order a poor man around because the poor man is guaranteed of a minimum standard of living regardless of his politico-economical circumstances, in all Western democracies anyway.

This rise of modern human rights is no thanks to the conscience or charity of the elite class. It came through the participation of the underclass in wars, which used to be an exclusive preserve of the elite males and volunteering of able, misguided unprivileged men by default. Even as recent as WW I, commissions could be practically bought at shire regiments. The modern wars of industrial scales made it impossible to manage without full participation of entire nations. With it came leveling of grounds between the elite class and the underclass, i.e. obligations could not be imposed without any recompenses. Thus, the birth of modern democracy greatly owes to modern wars, and it is not a coincidence that Labour movements, suffrages and liberalism all gathered momentum around this time.

The strengthening human rights are not an overreaction to misconceived and misplaced sense of world crises and injustices, and reflect weakening nationhood CIs and are a precursor to a supra-national, borderless network CI supported by wider humanity replacing staatsräson.

The empowerment of individuals across the world is yet, however, without a proper global institutional guarantee as the strength of nationhood CIs is generally proportional to a degree of individuals' trust given over to the state. It is therefore not in the interest of the state to have to be subservient to any higher authorities to administer the issue of human rights. Human rights must be camouflaged under 'citizens' rights' for nationhood CIs. This becomes an issue because citizens' rights are variable based on how accommodating the state is, while human rights are perceived to be above the state and universal. Citizens' rights which are often traced back to Magna Carta are juxtaposed to the predecessor of nationhood CIs (i.e. sovereign power apparatus based CIs or kingdom CIs) and used to be really a protective clause of elite few powerful citizens and had little to do with common folks. On the other hand, the notion of human rights conceptually surpasses even nationhood CIs and is not something that should be cherished under the umbrella of nationhood CIs. It is something that would transform nationhood CIs.

UN is not yet the guarantor of human rights, nor US any nearer even to an implicit advocator of human rights, considering recent events like misguided revenge-motivated Iraq war, extraordinary rendition tortures, blatantly egoistic environmental policies and Snowden revelations, despite their habit of preaching the world about democracy and human rights. The demand for, and the necessity of legal receptacle for human rights, call for a higher global authority. It is a challenge even if US can take any initiative for it. The failure to be a moral leader befitting to the so-called democratic champion will lead to the loss of trust for US as the most dominant world leader. If US want to lead the world to a next stage of encompassment and remain a leading player, then it needs to metamorphose into the supra-national champion of human rights and transcends the interest of its nationhood CI.

It is citizens of the world replacing citizens of nationhood CIs calling for the protection of international laws in place of a national law. However, any current attempts of supra-national enforcement of justice in this regard are highly rudimental and fragmental from nation to nation. Think how difficult it would be to enforce human rights e.g. on China or Russia. Likewise, the notion of the crimes against humanity bases its authority on the concept of humanity CI although in terms of enforcement this humanity CI as yet lacks an institutional backbone and is heavily reliant on US goodwill as the world police, although it is often questionable if US really aspires to such a high moral authority.

Human rights issues represent a direction towards a CI which does not yet exist. The humanity CI is only a theoretical CI which has not fully established itself as a functioning encompassing CI. An encompassing CI needs to be inclusive. The humanity CI, being higher up in terms of encompassment, is also in near vacuum and provides little benefits to members. There is nothing special about being a human as everyone is. This means 'human rights' are not a tangible benefit but more a code of conducts for CIs to be encompassed by the humanity CI. So, why do we talk about the humanity CI as if it already exist? In reality many CIs that may potentially comprise the humanity CI are not fully inclusive. Nevertheless, we seem to set up the humanity CI as if to subjugate those non-inclusive CIs.

This is so because we are aware the era of nationhood CIs is entering a sea change and requires something higher to maintain an order at a time of such a historical evolution. Human rights and nationhood CIs are not necessarily in accord and sometimes exclusive. Mineckean staatsräson rules over human rights. By putting them together under the same humanity CI we are demanding nationhood CIs to change their characters so that we can together enter a higher encompassing CI. The talks of human rights are therefore not an ignorance of some idealistic Nordic nations and naïve politicians, more their unconscious wisdom to anticipate and prepare for something higher than nationhood CIs. It is for this reason we should not be unconcerned with the issues.

A higher encompassing CI implicit in human rights is also responsible for the movements towards devolution in some European nations. That is, this seeming contradictory increase in CIs is made possible because of the emergence of an even larger encompassing CI than the current nationhood CIs. It is the feel good factor in the safety of this higher CI that affords the break-up of a nationhood CI as medieval style invasions and incursions between nations are no longer believed. Nationhood CIs already lost their Mineckean sublime status in favour of this still uninstitutionalized higher CI. However, in the question of devolution the deciding factor is tangible benefits as it happened with Scotland. No devolution is viable if one gets worse off as a result, much as any expectations towards liberal democracy are coupled with desires for better benefits (a major reason why Arab Spring did not go well). Benefits creation is the core issue of any CIs. Catalonia may well be better off being an independent nation, being richer than the rest of Spain, if a full devolution is allowed. Devolution is also a sign of political weakness as witnessed through incompetent politicians and less powerful civil services.

7.4. Gender Issues

Herein, lies the primitive wedlock of fundamental concepts such as 'law,' 'society,' 'love,' 'money,' etc.. Cut through layers of complexities overlapped via psychology, economics, sociology, anthropology, etc.., a female is something that is more likely to be able to identify itself through a male and thus makes a demand on a male to acquire 'power' through the invention of 'CI.' Put it more vulgarly but penetratingly, a female is a commodity that wishes to be desired to be 'purchased' by a male whose currency is a barometer of strength that balances intelligence, physique, character, appearance and inheritance, and a CI is a means that allows all these factors to be translated into readily decipherable units of measure. For a female, a society is a law that forces males to purchase with universally acceptable currency rather than his own printed money. For a male, a society is a source of power yielded through a CI. Thus, it is in the interest of females to form a society, where males are governed (i.e. kept under a law) by acceptable codes of conducts by the creation of 'money' which transcends mere brutal forces and is accepted as hierarchy within a CI, and, all in all, a society is more beneficial for females. Females are intuitively aware societies are advantageous to them, and females see themselves as a commodity to be desired by males. This is why they bother to take time and trouble to make themselves attractive, to change their name if necessary, which is observed across many cultures, to make a male to think of a possession and thus to remind a male of his obligations to his possessions. At puberty many females become aware that it is a short cut to life's necessities to attract males who work for power than striving for powers themselves without knowing outcomes.

Put it more coarsely women's power is basically their presumed capacity to attract men, while men's power is an ability to excel over other men, ranging from manual skills and financial knowhow to scientific knowledge and abstract thinking, which are directly and indirectly monetarily translatable, and so that they can be attractive to women. It is thus women are usually (but not always) inferior in terms of mundane knowledge attainments and productions, and women are attracted to men because of men's proximity to power (with an element of social engineering).

In the horizontal world, female contributions to knowledge should increase and male contributions to decrease, but reflecting the less vertical nature of female mindsets and therefore of less competitive creative nature, net contributions will go down. Male socio-economic standings will see a dramatic downshift and more than equate rise for females because in a more female-orientated CI there is less room for vertically structured powers.

For most cases, a body is a tool of trade for female practicalities and is accordingly looked after like 'capital good' and in many cases it is an object of desire, or even of love, for a male mind. This natural but uneven advantage was historically brought to disadvantage by commoditizing female bodies by means of economic, legal and social deprivations, or shall I say, by medieval social engineering. Feminist corrections are well-meant but are also Pandora's Box that tips the balance towards females' natural favour and induce many unintended consequences primarily and paradoxically by widening gender gaps, at least provisionally. Economic and social equality enshrined in the law means less male desires for power and thus taking away motives for creativities (of lower kinds) and drives for economic achievements. The institution of marriage will have to go through fundamental reviews. All these also mean there will be reactions, not necessarily in females' favour. However, as mere four steamships caused the fall of the declining but still pretty solid power apparatus that lasted 250 years in 1853-1868 Japan, these subtle but steady power shifts will contribute to create a new society probably across national and religious boundaries, based on female eusocial natures. The Islamic religion appears to be putting up the last and doomed defense against these Amazon onslaughts.

The most primitive money is an assigned place in a society which enables the assignee legitimately to acquire various commodities including females by means of rights exercisable within that society as you might remember '*droit du seigneur.*' That is why money is even today almost synonymous with power, and for a long time females were kept away from it. This is not just a medieval fiction, but is rooted in primitive necessities of our existence, which may be alleviated through conventions as befitting improved plights of modern life, but will take no time to revert back to its dark origin given set-backs in socio-economic situations as is often seen in war scenarios even today. And much as any military cannot consist of identical ranks, money/power cannot be of parity to everyone. Therefore, if there is someone rich, there will always be someone poor.

So-called 'love' is, by its seeming genuineness, a catalyst that transforms this social process into an emotional process, thus greatly reducing relational energy needed for the process as emotional interactions often ignore formalities of social contracts. The basic relationship from a male to a female is, a 'love' of ownership that leverages his place in a CI, while the basic relationship from a female to a male is, a 'love' of self that finds a place in the power structure of a CI. Thus, great literatures are invariably based on the misunderstanding of a love between males and females. Male romanticism stems from mislaid, misplaced or lost ownership by fates, interventions of other males or his own stupidity, while female fatalism is expressed through pragmatism, dissatisfaction of self identified through inferior males or injustice of social bonds imposed upon female sex, i.e. secret grievances/revolts against imposers. A literature is composed on this misuse of a same word 'love' between females and males. For German romanticism, a 'love' is typically a male love, while for enlightened Victorian English female writers a 'love' is often a social indispensable. Typically, I recall Goethe for the former, and Jane Austen for the latter.

Put it more vulgarly, women are sellers, while men are buyers. Sellers need a merchandise to sell and a skill to market it. i.e. the merchandise is themselves in various forms. Some are fortunate to be in a ready-salable good form, some need to be complemented with better marketing. Skills vary from instinctive and intuitive appeals to acquired tactility augmented with education, knowledge, mannerism, etc.. Buyers need a currency in order to purchase. Put it extremely, while women are themselves walking merchandise, men are themselves nothing without money. Thus, men are generally at a disadvantage in terms of stress endurance. To complicate the matter more, under the current gender arrangement women can play a double game; they can try to play the equality card, while failing that they can always go back to the 'husband hunting' game with far more accommodating legal frameworks. It is this need of men to acquire power (largely translatable into money) that makes men more creative. Women, on the other hand, are themselves a ready-made commodity without much effort. Thus, men have innate necessity to strive. The upper-echelon of men are always more creative than any higher echelons of women, although they come no doubt higher than most plebe men. For some psychopathic and autistic men creativity is for its own sake, without any heeds to women. This type of male creativity can attain ethereal flight in thin air, while female creativity is, even at its height, almost always bound to the ground, i.e. down to earth by their bodily connections. Likewise, for lesser creative men sometimes money become its own end and enjoys accumulating it not for any social uses, but for its own sake. These are male inclinations initiated by their need to strive but so twisted that the means became its own end for sheer pleasure of it. Thus, geniuses are always men and it is not a coincidence that women do not produce any as their priority is their own bodily preoccupations. For most ordinary men and women neither is intellectually more superior to the other.

I do not know if there are such anthropological observations, but where feminine beauty is more pronounced, cultures are more creative. Where it is more repressed or hard to come by, creativity is limited or base. Examples contrary to this are hard to find. Islamic cultures, when more relaxed like Ottoman courtly life, used to be more creative not only in arts but even in science. If they should encourage feminine attractiveness and impose necessity to strive on males, Islamic cultures may become more creative again, even prosperous without oil. One could even go so far as to suggest that when cultures were more isolated, i.e. when males were less aware of the unattractiveness of their females, their cultures were more artistic and creative. Likewise, cultures of too accommodating females, of overt male dominances for whatever reasons, tend to be less creative. Wherever men are too comfortable, they have less reason to strive. It is for the sake of our spices females become attractive and stress males to be competitive. Or is this a fallacy of my vertically orientated thinking?

The loss of female innocence through empowerments is a double-edged sword; in that the process has just begun through male complacency and that the erosion of the status quo will lead to various repercussions which will affect existing power structures. It is not that the seeming progression of female rights might at some stage provoke male antagonism which was kept in check through the policy of social cohesion based on enlightened equality and bring about disadvantages which were thus far superseded by advantages. There is a case for that, but there is a far more serious implication on our existence through gender unification/neutralization. Assuming that the current gender shift has a deeper cause, not a mere claim for equality, this will demand to rewrite the whole power structure with which we are accustomed through centuries. First of all, much of our hierarchical orders are male orientated as can be typically observed in any male institutions like military or quasi-military organizations. The female empowerments are a far-reaching result of male misdemeanors over wars, which, with the advents of industrial technologies and counter-male-intuitively, turned out to be disastrous as against the kind of play-game wars which used to enhance male powers and prestige and keep females at bay in their demand for more powers through minor social disturbances. The kind of wars which can be turned into symphonies, poems or family sagas, were over with the arrival of industrial scale killings, which annihilated ruling males in the first instance and then diminished male powers in the second as males proved themselves incapable of protecting females, let alone themselves. Much as a change in male hierarchy was also brought about by the same misdemeanors, when sacrifices were forced on subjugated parties like working class males or females at large by the errors of ruling males, prices are required in terms of the loss of the status quo privileges. As I said, societies are more advantageous for females, and acceptable disruptions thereof used to confirm male superiorities. It is the current impossibilities of engaging in industrial scale wars that creates hitherto unseen peace (despite the opposite impressions given by the media) and the rise of female powers. Furthermore, there is also an element of biochemical processes that seem to reduce maleness and enhance femaleness across the world, i.e. hormonal feminization. In addition, we are also into an era of female demystification through better understanding of basic biology and psychology.

If this reduction in gender gaps is an irreversible long-term process, then we are into many surprises. Most of mediocre to low male creativity directly or indirectly centres on want of power to attract females. Gender neutralization naturally reduces this want. The human world will be thus poorer with creativity. Imagine D. H. Lawrence or Goethe without female ambience. Even Shakespeare will decidedly look odd with masculinized females and feminized males. Needless to say that many similar examples can be found in fine arts or even in sciences. Consumption patterns will change and demands for consumption may diminish if males care less to impress females and females mind less to be attractive. Not only service sectors dependent economies but eventually the whole global economy will slow down. What we observe in Japan, which has been a reliable forward indicator as symbolized by e.g. economic 'japanification' of disinflationary traps coupled with crippling national debts or cultural 'japanization' of sushi, computer games and mangas, is not just socio-economic phenomena but also a gender issue. Not only males care less for females but empowerments positively put them off. This is compounded by self-fulfilling prophecy of declining birth rates and consequently aging demography. No wonder there is no way out for that country (except by female empowerments as mentioned elsewhere). Incidentally in the over-populated, catastrophes-prone world dwindling but well-regulated nations are in for favour. Not withstanding current problems a smaller Japan is a correct solution for them although the transition is a painful one. More insidiously, if a hierarchical society is of male character stemmed from desire for power, female empowerments mean a less monetized society much as the rise of social securities reduced the power of money. It is not the sum of money but its distribution that create the social usefulness of money. However, the less monetized society is not necessarily replaced by a more peaceful society. Money is the most important governing tool of society ever discovered. Displacement of money without a substitute may mean a disorder that brings about male uprisings, an interesting civil war, so to speak.

Interestingly and contradictorily, the currently condemned male characters of the Islamic world is, by merits or defaults, the results of their largely having stayed out of catastrophic wars (the kind that wiped out literally tens of millions, not little ones here and there) and the Western condemnations are misplaced in the sense that it is not their wisdom that gave freedom to females but rather male stupidity that empowered females. Just observe how grudgingly males acceded to female demands of suffrage and only after discovering the unstoppable momentum more and more males patronizingly pretended to be gracious in giving in to female demands, which continues to this day. As the working class gained ground after the sacrifices of WW I, which, by tradition, should really have been a conduct of so-called elite males only, females finally won over men after two WWs' worth of male mischief. There is nothing so-called Western men can scorn Islamic men about, who just happened to be more peaceful and consequently managed to maintain their *status quo* longer than Western men. The Western world is fearful of the Islamic world partially because of this anomaly in gender gaps and wants to bring down the Islamic men to their level, so that there is a level playing ground, i.e. cultural cohesion, across the world. Seeing this from an Islamic perspective this is adding injury to insult, although looking from the Western standpoint this is yet another example of Islamic backwardness. I will leave it for history to judge except saying that East/West relationship resembles to Male/Female relationship and females are on the rising. All I say is the current gender neutralization has yet a long way to go, together with many unexpected hazards. It may turn out it is females who have more to lose. However, the rise of females is a peace dividend and is an established trend for now.

For a male, love is a temporary suspension of self-identity and is a momentary anomaly. This means the loss of CI as a CI cannot be drawn without 'self' at the centre. Marriage is a social convention to substantiate this anomaly as a contract for the benefits of a female. This state of affairs was tolerated even though the contract was inherently flawed in favour of males. Males had more possessions like money, property and jobs. Marriage is a token gesture if the contract can be reneged without serious monetary penalties. The current move to upgrade this contract as full-blown equality of possessions will deter males to commit the folly of giving a permanent feature to their temporary loss of sanity.

Marriage matters more for females because a female tends to have a male as a CI if its Freudian ego is better served by doing so, and for a male it is alchemy of turning a temporary privilege into a permanent obligation. In a good old-fashioned way, a female may have a much simpler scheme of CI. If one is happy to be provided with all the ego necessities by a male, then one can be contented with having that male as the only CI. However, this simpler life form is being replaced with a gender-free life form by females' desire to be independent. Whether this can produce a happier outcome or not, is yet to be seen.

Gender equalization and stigma-free society mean less creativity. Generally speaking a happier environment induces less creativity. We are entering a less creative stretch of history, although prolonged happiness has a propensity to destabilize itself as we would rather be more creative and enjoy the freedom of thoughts and actions despite the discomfort of unhappiness. Historically, we were always more creative (and men ruled over women) at a time of instability as typically observed e.g. at the time of Renaissance. In our time of peace and stability, be it Monte Cristo, Larson trilogy, Slumdog Millionaire, Queen of South, etc. the most eternal successful formula for so-called creative arts like fiction, drama and film is the combination of the personal sufferings at the hands of injustice, the acquisition of fortunes through ingenuity and luck and finally the most delicious revenge. The more extreme and clever the plots are, the greater the appreciation they enjoy. The morale of this eternal formula is that we like disliking injustices and enjoy applying our creativity (of a lower kind) to effect our natural sense of justice. But, for us to be able to enjoy this privilege there have to be injustices, to start with. Likewise, it is only natural for females to expect fairness in gender issues, but males revolt in this lukewarm feminine happiness as it deprives them of the pleasure of being more creative and competitive.

Attempts to equalize genders by means of laws and regulations may be doing superficially the right thing, but will have repercussions, e.g. on the economy. Take out various elements of gender in the most vigorous way from an economy, and it will lose half its momentum. Male CI and female CI are over-lapping, not exclusive because of the encompassing humanity CI. A la de Beauvoir females are not born, but a creation of hormonal metamorphosis coupled with cliché-based social engineering. As we realize the mechanism, biological, psychological and social, of how a female tuned woman is made, the ancient myth of womanhood disappears like a puff, and a woman becomes a man half empty, as much as a man, a woman half full. The gender equalization is the question of the removal of cliché, i.e. of given rights and acquired benefits, a matter of reverse social engineering of ignoring each other's gender. It is the disparity, display and even exaggeration of gender that encourages lower end of creativity and various commercial activities symbolized in consumption and contributes to the wealth creation under our current economic model. The gender equalization must be net positive to offset these considerable socio-economic disquiets.

Like medicine (not medical science), which does such a service to mankind but may be doing a long-term disservice by weakening natural physiological capacity, e.g. through inappropriate, widespread uses of antibiotics or by interfering with evolutionary processes (but we cherish medical science because it leaves us with our options open), the removal of gender issues from our social consciousness may be political correctness carried too far based on the outcries of a few activists and the silence of lazy majorities. On the other hand, given gradual adjustments without upsetting our socio-economic boat too much female empowerment is inevitably part of 'horizontalization' of CIs and, in some idiosyncratic cases, may bring benefits of rejuvenating waning nationhood CIs without waiting too long, provided the host CI is intellectually and emotionally ready. I already mentioned such a possibility for Japan.

Rhetorically speaking, women exist for humanity, most men exist for women, a few men (men for whom power rightly or wrongly becomes its own end, and not for the sake of anything else, including women) represent humanity, a very few men expand the boundary of humanity through intellectual rigours, which women have practically no needs to possess. When a young pretty face and/or healthy body, or even failing those, taciturn and tactile manners do the trick of acquiring 'benefits' without going through the torture of intellectual rigours with no promises of any benefits in many cases, why should women bother even challenging men in this sphere (although one must always allow some exceptions). This is probably where men and women differ most greatly. In the days of gender equalization, I do not know what empowerment does to such a biologico-psychological issue. If empowerment means duties in return for rights in full scale (i.e. no 'pick and choose'), then it will come to strong resistance from a large section of women folk. There are many benefits and merits they will have to forgo in return for many rights they may acquire. Gender equalization will have many unforeseen pitfalls, which we probably have no choice but to go through.

7.5. Religion

Religions are primarily bonding principles to form CIs. It is more than a coincidence that in religious circles often familial terms like father, mother, son, brother, sister are used to denote fellowship relations. Religions, even the most dogmatic ones, therefore have a convenient capacity to evolve in order to follow suit the fashion of times. The interpretations of so-called 'holy texts' accommodate the needs of periods. I need not elaborate this by citing the accommodation of homosexuals, females, contraception, sainthood, even suicides, etc., in order to appease the fashionable views. The developments of religions are full of these examples. Coupled with bonding principles are tools of trades that are ceremonies and organizational hierarchy. They together appease psychological needs of people who participate in these CIs. Religious CIs are today rather lacking in tangible benefits and are therefore in particular needs of psychological benefits. Through the offer of fellowship religious CIs can be therapeutic and tend to appeal to vulnerable people.

A religion became such an easy label to put on anything from daily description of oneself to terrorism because it gives and takes little benefits in today's world and because it is such an easy subject for narrative discourses as it is referenceless and defies any objective analyses, in short, fit for simple souls. Religions, in these contexts, practically mean nothing, be it Muslim fundamentalists or Christian terrorists. One should not try to see more in them than what they really are. Religions here are just borrowed names for tactless glorifications for petty violence. There is nothing holy in any violence in any religions.

It is too simplistic to view Muslim culture as backward and so-called Western culture as progressive through e.g. the treatments of gender issues. It is a historical coincidence that the Western culture accommodated suffragettes a mere century before the Muslim culture is currently faced with. This does not testify that Western culture is more enlightened or righteous. It is for the want of equal grounds for socio-economic reasons or psychological satisfactions or even fears that the Western culture try to enforce its views on the gender issues on other cultures.

Applying the scheme of CI, one can see an example of the strong inclusive CI in the inclusive relationship of a community CI wrapped in a religious CI. As it stands, this is still the case with the Muslim culture at large. For various historical reasons like relatively less corruption of priesthood due probably to less hierarchical and less centralized power structure (for contrast, remember the history of Renaissance popes), no radical separation of state and religion and less educational developments, many Muslim societies are often a community as well as religious CI in tandem. This gives some fearful impressions of their cultural resilience. On the other hand, the Christian world took a different historical course. The early Christian society was probably more inclusive and strong in terms of inclusively wrapped CIs of religion and community as one might still see such examples in the likes of isolated Coptic and Syriac communities. However, as states, churches and leading families developed their sphere of influence, their inclusive relationship deteriorated and weakened the early inclusive CI into exclusive/overlapped and less cohesive CIs. This gave rise to more liberated societies with looser relationship under a larger encompassing CI and provided us with so-called democratic sense of freedom. This does not mean any superiority of the so-called western culture, but it is a result of historical coincidence due to too strong churches, stronger still of the developments of statehood based on large economic surpluses and a higher level of education observed through scientific advancements. All these contributed a stronger separation of state and religion.

The Western world needs to realize this historical diversion of cultural developments before trying to enforce their social values on the Muslim world. As it happened in their own history, the best course would be education, cultural encompassment through mutual-transformation, dilution and separation of religion and politics. It is not fear but patience that is needed in order to fill the gap of two hundred years, which translate into twenty years in today's timescale.

Religious CIs, through tangencies and encompassments, come to represent many issues of the day for their survival. Theological adjustments, gender issues, even extremist views, they are all tentacles of religious CIs seeking higher grounds for next stages of encompassment. It should be noted, however, that fascist CIs or extreme religious CIs of any denomination do not have any scope for great expansion because they will be excluded by excluding others. It is the lack of ability to encompass and is, therefore, against the laws of CI that they prosper. Given time, they either disappear or get dissipated into a more encompassing CI.

The fear of terrorism tends to be overplayed as a decoy for politicians to shift their incompetence and decline of importance onto something so easy to blame and at the same time to enjoy media attention in their guaranteed favour. There is an element of cry for help in extremisms. Starved of any tangible benefits internally and externally their CIs are in perpetual decline. Extremists are products of excluding/excluded CIs which can only seek tangency for encompassment in violence. Violence is a form of communication for someone incapable of communication. If politicians can physically eliminate terrorists, that is an easy solution. However, if they cannot for whatever reasons, then providing them with an environment where their CIs can see a way for encompassment like a corridor of escape is the only practical way. In our days of human rights, violence for violence generally fails to deliver cost effective solutions, especially for politicians of family business who lack street wisdom and world domineering spine.

Incidentally, much of religious orientations such as searches for 'God,' 'soul,' 'spirit,' etc.., stems from my Hypothesis 1. That is, each and every one of us as a part, seeks a whole, which is a CI and eventually leads to Ω at the end of encompassment processes. We name this (more a process than an object), which we have an innate necessity to form but do not have by ourselves, as 'God,' etc.. In other words, a timeless omnipresence of something absolute, 'God,' is more precisely intellectually economical non-entity, as we fail to see, but only 'feel,' a whole in ourselves and because Ω only appears at the end of on-going processes, as a CI.

So-called 'holy idiot' as appears in Karamazov, etc.., is a 'self' which lacks this necessity by default ,and we see a whole in this, which is a part that does not seek a whole, an imaginary CI dreamed by bystanders. That is, we see a whole in a part that is incapable of seeking a whole. Note 'holy idiot' can only be singular as it is an imaginary CI with only one member and cannot be any more inclusive.

7.6. Science

Scientists are perceived to be people who engage in empirical pursuits of rules of nature and are members of communities who share some common languages of which entry level proficiency is deemed to have been reasonably achieved at PhD. These languages always contain a level of mathematics which ensures communality among speakers. That is the rules of numbers are a common grammar of scientific language. The tools of science are the mathematical grounds which allow so-called scientists to formulate and communicate ideas and respective hypotheses that are commonly assumed within each confine of the scientific fields. It is the knowledge of these tools of science that forms the scientific CI. Outside of the domain of particular scientific language scientists are also free to engage in any irrational pursuits as it often happens. Being a scientist does not guarantee someone is always intellectual and intelligent, or even rational. There were and are many so-called scientists with religious convictions, Newton included, although I would give him an allowance of a historical era when religions prevailed over every corner of our life. Someone is a scientist and intelligent only in so far as he is proficient in his adopted language and speaks about things which are within the domain of the subject matters of his chosen language. A good scientist is someone who can expand this scope of his language, like a good novelist who enriches his chosen common language. Therefore, needless to say that just because someone is a recognized scientist and speaks about something beyond the scope of his language as if he knows about this something, this something does not have any scientifically recognized ground. This is often the case with so-called celebrity scientists of our days, who tend to speak aloud on too many subjects on which they are not well qualified to do so.

Likewise an applied science is a language which proved to work when adopting rules of nature onto practical modeling so as to project human values in nature. Therefore, in the world of one nano-second ± Big Bang (assuming there was one) it is highly debatable if this forms part of nature where science can be applicable. Beyond logic and mathematics, there is no empiricism in such a world. It is also beyond these tools to look into the tools themselves, the retrogression of which results in yet another tool. Beyond the mathematical language themselves, science always assumes the indescribable. Take these language away and science becomes a quasi-religion. There are too many things so-called scientists do not know to be able to complacently affirm of their supremacy of achievements and methodology. Physicists cannot even describe 95% of the components of the universe according to their own standard view. Many so-called scientists (of lower caliber) are often blind, arrogant and stubborn in the assumptions of the supremacy of their methodologies and forget that they too are confined within their tools of trade, i.e. their languages. Only those who experienced necessities of inventing a new language know how intimately connected are a tool of description and objects or states of affairs they wish to describe. Sometimes, it is even the case that one invents/discovers/describes what one is destined to invent/discover/describe in the cul-de-sac of a given language. This is especially true of pure mathematics where the tool of description and the objects of description are interconnected and entwined at the most abstract end.

Scientific language makes assumptions which at various levels have to be taken for granted, until a coherent challenge may lead to the construction of a new language. However, science, especially pure science, is a long way from being exhaustive and does not deliver any complete pictures of any given fields of the world, let alone of the world itself. Accordingly, we do not yet possess the one and only common language of science. Not only each language of science has severe restrictions within its paradigm, and, since we do not have any general language of science, we are unable to afford a comprehensive review of its achievements and future paths. There are, in fact, many incomplete branches of the incomplete languages of scientific attempts. At the frontier of scientific investigations, two scientists can be two strangers dealing with a same subject-matter if they fail to share a same assumption.

Thus, it is too premature even to think that in near future physics can deliver a coherent full explanation of how our universe started, or even started at all, and where we stand today.

There are two ways of engaging in science. One is to start with its language, a mathematical language of a science and often end up as its captive. The other is to start with extra-linguistic insights and acquire a linguistic skill in order to express them. The latter tends to be founders of scientific paradigms. A language of science is necessarily mathematical, but this is only a necessary condition. Confined within you are only scientific engineers. To be necessary and sufficient, you need a talent that goes beyond its language, just like a composition genius. Acquiring the skills of composition does not make him a good composer. You need poetic intuition and inspiration. In our age, too much emphasis is on the acquisition of linguistic skills as scientific language becomes more refined and complex and fails to touch upon poetic insights as the former is educationally much easier and the latter is difficult, if impossible, to teach. Mediocre scientists are speakers of scientific language and mere engineers, while a good scientist is metaphorically a poet. There is a confusion of acquiring linguistic skills and being a scientist and often the former is confused with the latter. As one often ends up only acquiring part of a still developing scientific language, acquiring linguistic skills does not itself make someone a scientist, or even a rationalist. Proudly calling oneself a scientist and presumably implying being rational, is more likely a sign of being a simple soul. One does not grow into a scientist, instead, one is made a scientist by acquiring language of science typically via school curricula.

Although one does become a so-called scientist by acquiring a certain level of a relevant language, together with a methodology implicit in the grammar and semantics of that language, linguistic skills are a double-edged sword. On the one hand, you have a command of skills to understand and represent chosen subject-matters. On the other hand, you could be easily swallowed up and lost in linguistic intricacies as this is a language invented, refined and inherited by many generations of excellent brains, maybe many times superior to learners themselves. If lucky, you probably end up refining some linguistic aspects without realizing you are still within the linguistic confines. Or worse still, you could be a scientist, but you could be as superstitious as a girl next door, apart from your mathematical skills, which does not really give you any extra profound knowledge, apart from superficial representational skills and satisfactions.

The acquisition of a language only allows you to see things within that language and discuss about things which have been conceptually fully incorporated in that language. It is only poetic intuitions that take you beyond linguistic skills and see and hear things that are denied within that language and inspire you to expand that language to include a new scope. These poetic insights only come from your awareness of being part of a totality which many languages try to explore, each in its own way, but cannot deal with together without forming yet another language. This totality, however, has to be an intellectual totality to be appreciated and expressed schematically in order to be intelligible. It might be poetic, but a science has to be embodied in a schematic representation. It is only superficial aspects of science that call for empiricism; at mathematical limits even science makes many nonempirical assumptions. It is superficial scientists, i.e. someone only with linguistic fluency, who are contend with mathematical analyses of a narrow spectrum of chosen events.

A language of science is a tool of description. It is designed, improvised and refined to describe specific objects and in specific ways. These objects are not only of specific nature, but also of specific spectrums. There are many languages of science, but there is no general language of science to unite them all, other than some very basic communal areas. That task falls on philosophy as scientists are today specialists by nature. A same object may be described differently by different languages. A language so designed also so describes. The range and structure of a language may predetermine the way an object is chosen and described just like some ordinary language is more poetic and some more analytic by nature. Some scientific discoveries are made 'linguistically' by following logic and mathematics inherent in that language, i.e. by idealization, like many discoveries in the best formulated language of science, mathematics, or Galilean falling objects and Newtonian apples. Schrödinger's wave equation and subsequent attempts of interpretations are good examples of a language over the (unattached) world. It was inevitable that the Copenhagener observer becomes part of the observable event, be it via the collapse or the multi-worlds.

Science as a linguistic communality consists of two levels; at a basic level there is physical science, where their main occupation is modeling of immediate environments in order to replicate its mechanism for human benefits and to project human values onto nature, in another word a tool for human colonization of nature. Scientists at this level are language users or notational engineers. At a higher level, it is metaphysical science, where they are language explorers or paradigm designers. Here, scientists are philosophizing intellectuals who indulge in creative pursuits and pleasures of abstract thinking at the frontier of, but within communality of, the grammar of a scientific language.

Since science is of necessity the acquisition of linguistic skills and of sufficiency serendipitous inspirations and today requires the supports of engineering, it is also community-orientated. The science CI is, therefore, more and more a community CI by benefits and affinity where one acquires linguistic skills and cultivates team spirits. For funding needs, it is also closely associated with nationhood CIs. Although one sometimes dreams of a scientist as a Newtonian solitary genius, who only needs a pen and paper, today's scientists are much more likely mediocre team-players heavily reliant on equipments. Their languages are constantly refined and elaborated by immense manpower that it is not like Newton's days to rewrite or invent the languages of science single-handedly.

Combined with their propensity for social recognitions and monetary rewards, one would hope their CI would escape from parochial tendencies.

Away from geniuses, who have privileges of being left alone with pen and paper, ordinary scientists are members of the scientific community CI. 'Scientist' being a speaker of a language of science and there being no language of science with universal coverage and depth their community, CI is at best weak except when they share a small conclave of shared area of language. At superficial levels, it is in their mutual interest to form a community CI as science requires funding and team-work for their more and more engineering-orientated approaches. Their CI can liaise with nationhood CIs, corporate CIs, etc., for ease of funding and social recognition. This is where universities come in. Sciences incorporated in university education and organizations are at all levels used to cultivate a CI where they evaluate each other as scientists, of which benefits are mutual recognition as speakers of scientific language, and endow each other tangible benefits as befitting teachers of such languages endowed with practical socioeconomical benefits.

7.7. EU

EU is the first major attempt to create a non-imperial supranational sovereign region since imperialism took deep root in 18th century. It is, however, more of a bureaucratic process backed by democratic consensus, rather than a central policy rooted in national politics. All beneficiary states in current crises of EU, despite of various rhetoric, preferred the CI of EU to their own sovereign national CI. This proves that EU is successfully establishing a larger CI by providing more benefits to its citizens than being members of each sovereign state CI.

Beneficiary states have little qualm in appraising EU, while they are benefactor states that decide the fate of EU as a CI. The exporting state like Germany is actually a beneficiary of EU in a longer term and is patient and well off enough to take a long and strategic view, which seems to culminate in subsidizing France (via Agricultural Policy) so as to be the twin pillars of EU in tandem. The services and property orientated state like UK find it hard to see many benefits especially in a short term. UK politicians, being notoriously pragmatic as they are, will find it difficult to sell the idea of EU as a CI. However, the prosperity of UK owes much to its intangible characteristics; its language as the most commonly used tongue, the perceived fairness of its judiciary system and its political stability play an important role to place UK as a safe and trustable option for international investors. Therefore, it is vital for UK not to betray its well perceived image by playing any nationalistic card. That is, although UK has a renowned brand CI as world's trusted citizen, this CI goes in tandem with an encompassing CI so long as the latter is also perceived in trust by the world at large. UK should work with EU to create the image of an inclusive encompassing CI, not any nationalistic CI.

For the likes of Germany and other major EU countries much in debt to Germany in various subsidies the shortcoming of direct benefits will be compensated by perceived long-term benefits and will see it worthwhile to trade their respective national CI for that of EU as they are also the builders of CI of EU. UK who lacks German subsidized benefits, who also run large trade deficits with EU and who is a large net contributor of EU budgets, is in a more subtle position as their benefits are more intangible. On the one hand, playing a too nationalistic card to go it alone outside EU may damage its image of fair and safe haven of international capital. On the other hand, making use of EU to enhance the image of its CI might inevitably compromise its standing without very skillful maneuvering. Whether UK possesses such a grand political skill is an open question.

EU is still more of an experiment than an established fact of affairs. It is the first and only attempt thus far to try to establish a brand new CI out of existing and well-established nationhood CIs. Its success hinges on whether it can truly replace constituent nationhood CIs and incorporate various forward looking concepts mentioned elsewhere in this essay, such as the new media as political tools to harness horizontal forces, complete institutional gender neutralization, human rights as politico-economical constant to curve vertical power structures and above all a new paradigm of non-consumptive economic model. Their successful implementations will place EU not only as a higher new CI, but also as a pioneering encompassing CI towards Ω, and mankind as a whole would have so much to be grateful to this brave new CI.

It is significant in the sense that it contrasts with devolutionary movements elsewhere, although I mentioned the reason for such movements is really foretelling the coming of a new CI. It is also highly praiseworthy that EU seems to conform to a benevolent nature necessary to transcend nationhood CIs. It, however, still has many obstacles to achieve its goal, such as self-preserving instincts of nationhood CIs as becoming more and more obvious especially in the case of UK, historically a most pragmatic nation of merchants. So much still depends upon the goodwill of Germany. Whatever historical coincidences and geo-political necessities may have prompted EU, EU is no longer a consequence of the past, it is a great step forward towards a new encompassing CI hitherto unseen in our history. It is interesting to observe and honoured to participate in this monumental event. It would be such a pity if UK, an intelligent nation, should fail to remain in, and contribute to, this great experiment. EU should make every possible effort to retain UK, which is full of practical wisdom, cultural wealth, historical continuity and its leverage with US and English speaking world, not to mention its military value, so unlike any continental nations. UK is a vital ingredient of the success of EU, especially so because it has a strong sense of nationhood CI and its successful integration will further the victory of EU.

Short-term positive effects on beneficiary states borne out by the matching negative effects on benefactor states cannot last unless this bears long-term positive effects to all parties concerned. There is also a risk of wealthier nations' sucking out indispensable talents out of poorer states, which then become poverty traps to nurture criminalities and extremisms and become breeding grounds of EU's future problems. This will be compounded by linguistic inequilibrium affecting population movements. The union therefore must be economical as well as political, and more skewed towards the former the better. What hinders progress is languages, cultures and many differences in governing systems of member states, which are not just matters of laws, taxes and social benefits but also include more subtle but stubborn social customs such as corruption (remember institutionalized tax avoidance in Greece, from the very top to the bottom, originating probably to the days of Ottoman occupation), prejudices (as demonstrated by unfair national stereotypes in much popular press in benefactor states and aversion in the former Eastern Block countries towards refugees), wide-spread inner manipulative CIs of politico-criminal nature (mostly in the ex-Communist block). These will make it difficult for EU to consolidate into homogeneous, equal, open and transparent unity of soup. Much still depends upon the goodwill and patience of benefactor nations. EU needs to consolidate in order to have a stronger CI. It is the numerical benefits of CI reduction and parametric grouping toward H that provide the long-term more permeating benefits for EU, if EU can persevere the current on-going pains.

Although the current trend of decentralization in Europe and so-called 'democratization' of North Africa and Middle East seem contra-indicative, it actually confirms the existence of a larger CI in formation. It is on the back of the implicit safety fallbacks in the form of world opinions for human rights and possible US/EU ((wrongly) in the image of a vague precursor to the expected larger CI) back-up that encourage the likes of Scotland, Catalonia, some Balkan nations to try to go it alone, and that Arab uprisings against despots to call for US/EU interventions even when despots were often in liaison with US, if not wholly, then for geo-political marriage of convenience. They want to have their own independent CIs not because they geo-politically and economically deserve it, but because they feel safe enough to be protected by this yet unfathomed new and larger CI against the antagonism of the existing dominant CIs. That is, they see themselves encompassed and enfolded as CIs by this larger CI. This is a psychological luxury to play a CI game. E.g. that is why in contrast to England's lingering antagonism towards EU Scotland is always decisively pro-EU, and Arabs deliberately confuse political issues with religious issues so that in the bargain basement of powers they can barter risk for return under the shadow of real and fictitious CIs, i.e. where cash/gold is the only CI, this looming unfathomed CI is a good currency to trade with even to buy a tangible power of corruptions. Devolution and pseudo-democratization are cheap politics by cheap politicians for power games. Decentralizations seem to bring forth more CIs, but only because of fewer encompassing CIs that enable such decentralizations.

Entrenchments of human rights, the gender equalization and the new media, etc.., will contribute to the horizontalization of a nationhood CI. Nationhood CIs will be then less of a vertical power structure. We are not the ones who exist for nationhood CIs, but it is nationhood CIs that should serve us as it is we who created them. Nationhood CIs came into existence because they brought benefits for us to start with. However, a la Meinecke nationhood CIs became their own end assigned with a divine status and deliberately created tensions among themselves so that we became servants of nationhood CIs as if the loss of a nationhood CI would be our own destruction. The horizontalization of nationhood CIs is the destruction of nationhood CIs in the sense that it will gradually dismantle their borders, and we will see a higher and wider encompassing CI. EU could be a forerunner of this CI at least in spirit.

The horizontalization of a nationhood CI will create a new parametric of CI like $\forall$- and Λ-type. As a type of CI, it tends to produce fraternization and therefore groupings like $\forall$- and Λ-grouping, so is this new parametric. Horizontalized CIs will tend to group and initially give rise to socio-economic, psychological and political benefits, etc.., as new mindsets empathize with each other. They will eventually merge and form a single horizontal CI as becoming borderless is a characteristic of horizontal CIs, unlike vertically structured CIs. If this is a logical process, then, it can only be for practical benefits that we participate in the process, and not for any ideal's sake as it proved unworkable again and again. That is, why despite of various pitfalls, I can think of I generally agree with e.g. the gender equalization. We are only at the verge of a genuinely equalized society, but without any tangible benefits for all concerned this will not progress. However, if the horizontalization of a CI is logically inevitable, then the gender equalization will bring about net positive benefits for males and females alike.

Japan is likely to survive as a nationhood CI longer than most other CIs. It is precisely for this reason that it is likely to miss out playing important roles in this new CI, unlike multi-cultural, -ethnic, -linguistic and -religious US-UK. This is where UK differs from a similar island nation like Japan, which, though stable, remains an insular CI culturally and geo-politically. Japan is far too distinct and independent to be enfolded by US as an inclusive encompassing CI, although mutual trust is developing. This trust will have to undergo serious tests more than once. In this respect, all Far Eastern nations will fail the coming CI.

Although I am convinced of vital roles US-UK will play in the formation of a horizontal CI, it is the EU that could kick-start the process because of its entrenched human rights, experience of enfolding many sovereign nations successfully and, above all, precisely the lack of ambition for the global hegemony. Once the EU gets over its current crises and consolidates its socio-economic bases fully and hopefully and crucially succeeds in bringing in such a distinctly non-European nation like Turkey at some stage in future, the world will reappraise EU over US and give it a springboard to lead world opinion. The lack of ambition for global hegemony will act as a distinct advantage over US, which, with or without recent unsavory events like unscrupulous eavesdropping on heads of friendly nations and indiscriminate individuals exposed by Snowden and the suppression and persecution of WikiLeaks, unnecessarily tends to antagonize friends and foes alike.

For politically imperialistic and mono-cultural or culturally exclusive nations like China, Russia and others, even including some $\forall$-type nations, it is a non-starter even to think of encompassing other nationhood CIs, no matter how big their population or geographical size may be, or rather because of its domineering size combined with the nationalistic nature of their cultural psyche.

8. Future as a Logical Consequence

A CI not identified and strengthened in relation to other CIs, but a CI in itself, so to speak, is the most encompassing final CI. This is yet unknown to us and is only expressed as $\Omega \rightarrow \sim\Omega$. This is a CI without benefits, other than preference for existence, and there are no more tangency and encompassment processes to guide its *raison d'être*. It is an end product of benefits creation and being all encompassing there are no more CIs to derive and enhance benefits from for its members. Its organizational benefits are invisible since there is nothing that contrasts the significance of any benefits until their disappearance. Its benefits are taken for granted like the air we all breathe. Even a non-CI member enjoys its benefits as they permeate our space of modality.

However, as this final CI in vacuum can only contrast with itself in the form of negation and as we extrapolate our preference for existence rather than non-existence simply because we already exist and find it easier to maintain status-quo rather than venturing into the unknown, the problem is simply whether such a CI has a centripetal force to maintain its identity. We exist in order to exist. Our whole existence is to safeguard our existence. Our resources and knowledge is to ensure this purpose through cosmic catastrophes, beyond time and space. This is a call for intellectualism. We, who seek benefits, primarily tangible but including psychological and imaginary ones, for ourselves in order to be members of a CI, are forced to realize that it is a CI in itself that eventually goes into failover mode to resuscitate any defunct states of ourselves through the lack of visible benefits. Intellectualism is to eliminate the pettiness that motivates our daily existence, to remind us of our ultimate purpose. It commands higher regards for knowledge and above all values knowledge over excess material needs and despises greed to feed the desire for power that deviates from the above purpose.

All knowledge is respected, but for the purpose of existence it is ultimately physics (to understand the nature of physical world), biochemistry (to understand the origin and process of life), and engineering (that can materially translate any results of the above two and ensure the survival of earth-bound life form), which are required. All other disciplines are subsidiary to the above, and economics and politics are to balance our resources for the best possible duration to maximise the best possible attainment of our knowledge. Anything else helps to enrich and prolong our existence.

As CIs follow their laws, it is a logical consequence that they move up from lesser CIs to more and more encompassing CIs. For a more familiar future, the advent of internet accelerates the disintegration and transformation of the currently dominant nationhood CIs. The sovereignty of nationhood CIs is already weakening due to deepening networking within and beyond national borders. Likewise, our minds are merging due to entwinements based on the new media (with a consequence of less creativity). This is an encompassing process from nationhood CIs to a yet unnamed higher inclusive CI and eventually to the world CI and will present new and weaker shapes of nationhood CIs. The current devolution of some nationhood CIs should not be mistaken for the absolute strengthening of regional or local political powers but rather the relative weakening of nationhood CIs on the back of the emergence of a newly networking higher CI combined with, and supported by, the appearance of some supra-national CIs, typically EU, but including other regional supra-national alliances in Asia, Africa and South America. Also, some gender-based CI like feminist world alliance contributes the decline of old-fashioned nationhood CIs. The eventual World CI will finally transform into the Earth CI, given the encompassment of all earth-bound life forms by the Humanity CI. This, however, will have to wait some cosmic cathartic events that remind us we are all in a same boat.

The new media, like the steam engine centuries ago, is a game-changer and will bring about most profound changes unimaginable today. The advents of the steam were catastrophes for many who failed or refused to recognize its potential, from small examples of the Sudanese Dervish army against Kitchener or the American Indians' plights much hastened and worsened by Union Pacific to all those who ended up colonized by industrialized imperial powers. The British Empire was built on railways and steamships. Likewise, this is the beginnings of an important new era and like the age of the steam, those who embrace its potential to the full against all odds and disgruntlement will be the core of the new CI. Although we already feel too familiar with the new media, this is only a beginning and more serious effects are culturally, politically, socio-economically yet to come.

I say beginnings because the new CIs will probably come from hitherto unforeseen, unimagined and, no doubt more feminine, mindsets (and more and more merging mind) created from the propagations of the new media, rather than mutated nationhood CIs or some revolutionary social media. We only had less than 20 years of this new phenomena starting from the very basic internet, and it will take a few more generations to produce new species of mentality. Just as nationhood CIs produced nationally crazed (literally; even today some people are prepared to die for it and, worse, are admired for it) mentality (see Meinecke) unimagined in preceding centuries and created new wars, arts and sciences, the coming new mentality will produce many waves of unforeseen CIs and creativity (but generally less, I fear), good and bad. It will be interesting to see if this new mentality unites cultures, religions, etc. or remains a source of schism. In 50 years, we will encounter new species of mankind in terms of mentality unrecognizable today and almost alien to us, men of 20th century. If I venture to imagine, they will be much less individualistic in thoughts and deeds, more collective not necessarily in a negative sense, like eusocial animals I might add. This, combined with gender equalization in full acceleration, will produce mentally a new species. We will despise and admire them. Their CIs will be more akin to the final CI and we will be able to glimpse if we are just another evolved animals or something capable of approaching, dare I say from the lack of expressions, 'god,' which I am afraid will be nothing like a time-honoured Greek god.

From my limited observations of mankind, I tend to be inclined towards the former, yet it only takes one genius to compensate for the idiocy of 100 millions and one extraordinary talent to replace 1 million fools. The question is more if we as a whole can form a receptacle CI to fully embrace such idiosyncrasies. In history, who knows how many geniuses were stifled unwittingly by us. It is this intellectual quality of an encompassing CI that in the end matters. We are all responsible for it. This will decide if we are after all just animals (no offence meant for animals) or 'god' who may overcome an and all cosmic catastrophes. In conclusion, catastrophes and idiosyncrasies are the most deciding factors of history, not ordinary masses and linear trajectories of events. It is the ability of dealing with the unusual and unexpected that will save and preserve us, and our capacity as a CI to produce such abilities does matter. However, the cohesion of a CI does not often go hand in hand with the accommodation of idiosyncrasies. History may not be formed by geniuses, but certainly CIs that can produce geniuses are fundamental to it. It is the ability to embrace contradictions that wins history, like a Japanese sword.

There will be many who are reluctant to see the decline of nationhood CIs and, no doubt, there will be plausible reasons and excuses not fully to embrace the new media. However, it is a quality of good politicians to recognize the inevitable. This should involve the willingness of national politicians to incorporate the new media at every level of consultations and decision-making, accept their dwindling privileges and prestige and engage more and more bureaucracies beyond national borders like UN, EU or G7 or 8, wider regional defence cooperation instead of national military capabilities and accelerated free trades. The appearance of new media is having a quantum mechanical effect between an observer and an event. That is, informed members of a nationhood CI (voters) participate not only in the results of an event (elections), but also in its process. This should explain uncanny close results of recent elections of major nations. The new media empowers an individual to an extent that he starts voting not for his bona fide preferences, but for his own empowerments. The closer the election results are, the lesser the politicians are and the more powerful the voters are. This is a step towards a new CI via 'individuals vs nationhood.' This is a process that weakens nationhood CIs and strengthens individuals.

Nationhood-inspired events should be rebalanced by more borderless engagements and, to this end, events like Olympics and World Cup should be reorganized. Creative activities should be completely freed from nationhood CIs, which often provide funding as e.g. sciences and engineering require more equipments than brains today and arts are overcome by entertainments. Instead, they should be funded by supra-national organizations and results shared. Nationhood-induced dead-end will be replaced by creativity of a new dimension, and the next stage from nationhood CIs will gradually emerge. As the City of London and its various exchanges were originally founded on café networking, we may see some new institutions developing from the new media.

UN is more like an impoverished gentleman's club surrounded by opportunistic hand-out seekers, providing them with useful sources of minor corruptions for many small nations on one nation one vote system. For major donor nations, this is just a necessary cost of being a club member. UN has little power of CI, which is a sure sign as a failure. In fact, G7 or even NATO has a better and more useful sense of CI. The lack of leadership and proper governance makes it not the solution to the world's problems but itself a problem without a solution, like a village assembly which donors despise and beneficiaries cry out for more for nothing. It failed to create any effective sense of identity. For UN to be more useful it needs to be able to cultivate a CI. This cannot be done without a political will to dismantle the status-quo. This will, however, is currently non-existent owing to schism of givers and takers. No one will change unless there is something more for himself and, therefore, no one will agree for any changes. UN needs to reflect a wider power structure of the actual world, neither one nation one vote General Assembly nor post-WW II legacy veto-riddled Security Council are fit for purpose and outdated by today's realities. The former is not much more than a graduate school for trainee diplomats, the latter is an arcane poker-game which complicates rather than solves problems.

For UN to have any sense of CI, it has to be a stake-holders' institution, where everyone contribute in varying degrees and its decisions are binding by force. It also needs the strengthening of supra-national justice system with enforcement power, preferably with direct military capacity, paid for by all and sanctioned by all. The archaic power of veto should be abolished in favour of majority rules. Here, probably the biggest stumbling block is likely to be US whose authority has to be diluted in order to accommodate the new UN. But, as long as US is still expected to contribute the biggest proportion of budget and also, indirectly, military assets as the world's policeman, I see little prospects for this and UN remains the graveyard of nationhood CIs. It should try to harness democratic legitimacy through the use of social media as a step towards the world CI.

This state of UN is interesting to observe as a warning to any higher encompassing CIs above nationhood CIs. The reason why the current UN has no sense of CI is mismanagement on the one hand, i.e. it is viewed as a place, paid for by a handful of donor nations, to listen to whinges of poorer neighbours, or a place of communications sponsored by giver nations, where neither givers nor receivers are particularly grateful and moreover it cultivates sense of injustice because of powers of veto given to only a handful of nations for a reason no longer justifiable. On the other hand, its all-inclusiveness by way of one nation one vote regardless of relative weights and contributions is dysfunctional in the real world and, therefore, gives little tangible benefits to sponsor nations and not enough benefits to receiver nations as sponsors have no reasons to be generous.

It needs a radical transformation to give rise to any sense of CI, without which the current modes of physical presentations and costs are not justifiable except for the benefits of vote riggings for so-called UN diplomats from receiving nations, very much like old IOC and present FIFA officials. From this disgraceful and dysfunctional state of affairs for UN to progress into some sort of receptacle for an eventual higher encompassing authority, it first needs to develop a sense of CI, the first step of which will be to burrow into some existing CI like the humanity CI or world CI via some universally acceptable idea like human rights or environments and, above all, the acquisition of direct democratic mandates through the social media. Together with more democratic modus operandi and direct mandates UN should be called the World Council and empowered to endorse any major international positions.

It is ironic that US cannot rule the world so long as it remains a nationhood CI as its national regards will ultimately impede the borderless benevolence, as its national benefits will have to be diluted for the sake of the world, hence e.g. its egoistic attitudes towards the environment. US is an over-zealous, over-ambitious and over-extended nationhood CI which is aspired to become more than a nationhood CI, but does not know how to shed the mantle of nationhood. Although it extends its power beyond, and derives good part of its power from outside, its nationhood boundary, its nationhood status is a shell that, on the one hand, protects its power; on the other, limits its scope. It is idly passing precious transformative moments impotently. Likewise, UN has to remain a rather deliberate useless toy and not allowed to acquire any CI. US have power and motive to lead the world but, how can it destroy the shell of its nationhood CI that gives its citizens hegemonic benefits? The answer to it will be the shortest cut to the new CI, and here their politicians will be most severely tested. Otherwise, we have to wait the worldwide rise of new mindsets entwined into yet unknown unity by various social media, a structured horizontal force.

As a move towards the new encompassing CI, the above mentioned new mindsets should allow that any positions that have significant international influences, such as US presidency, the veto-powers of UN Security Council, leaderships of major nuclear powers, should have international components in their voting as well as direct participations of respective domestic citizens. International components consist in weighted sovereign votes for major nations. However, such changes will not be endorsed by our current narrow mindsets without some catastrophe as the status quo obscenely prevails otherwise.

Furthermore, I envisage that the language of this new CI will be English as it is the most widely used language across geography, cultures, religions, entertainments, politics, etc. That is also why US and UK will play a vital role in the next encompassing CI because a common language is an indispensable ingredient in the eusocial and supra-national nature of a higher CI.

It will be the process of horizontalization that allows the encompassment of nationhood CIs. As nationhood CIs become less and less vertically orientated, exchanges of people, money, ideas, cultures, etc.., become easier and nationhood CIs will be less distinct and more akin. In the reality of deepening global economy national economies are becoming less and less meaningful. Borders will go lower and lower and eventually disappear. This is already happening, although in the wrong name of 'Americanization' and combined with floods of legal and illegal migrations and more and more entrenched human rights. Parametric difference will remain an obstacle, but the wave after wave of horizontalization will force even the inner parasitic CIs to adapt to the new norm of the world, without which any benefits they are accustomed will shrink and dwindle like effects of invisible sanctions.

Horizontal CIs are silently and steadily already emerging, but it is the realization of the emergence of horizontal CIs that will put many dominant nationhood CIs on guard as they are destined eventually to take over any nationhood CIs. It is important for US to play along with this process, although it may eventually swallow US. After all, many values of a horizontal CI are democratic values and are already shared by most $\forall$-parametric CIs. The single utmost difference is a horizontal CI will dispense with vertical power structures as needs for tangencies and encompassments diminish. Horizontal CIs become closer to each other by parametric paradigm shift, not by tangencies and encompassments.

Nationhood CIs will give rise to regional horizontal CIs, where supra-governmental bodies will coordinate individuals via internet democracies. Nationhood CIs that guard their border by exclusion will face diminished benefits available to their members through parametric sanctions.

Horizontal CIs are eventually to form a single horizontal CI via parametric grouping. Thus, losers will be those in a position of influence in the vertical ladder of power transmissions. Potentially, they will be the biggest obstacle for the horizontalization, and no exclusive nationhood CIs will play an important role in the process.

The merged horizontal CI is still way off from the final CI in vacuum. In between lies the complete removal of vertical power structures, the extension of CI to the earthly life form (ideally any life form, assuming a common ground for all life forms throughout the universe), and further to the earth logic (ideally the structure of intelligence, assuming life culminates in intelligence, which has a common structure throughout the universe). What propels it from human benefits to benefits for life, and for intelligence, is the desire to secure our origin and achievements and may be termed 'intellectualism.'

The removal of vertical structures is necessary because they are what give a decisive edge to ego over superego. Ego is materially furnished with the ability to pursue its self-fulfilling, and eventually self-destructive, end by the vertical mechanisms of transmitting its will. The earthly life form; because that is where we sprang from, unless it has a 'ubiquitous and avuncular' cousins all over the universe. The earth logic, in case we do not survive in any biological forms; because that is the essence of life, the ability to view itself from the outside of itself or from above itself, as it were.

However, more down to earth, towards our immediate encompassing CI, science (objective knowledge) and great arts (I might say subjective knowledge with universality) all help harmonize CIs and enlarge the encompassing CI. That is, it is the lack of knowledge that allows for many varieties of CIs and non-inclusive relations of CIs. Thus, education is the key to a more encompassing CI, which will give rise to the common goal of the entire humanity, i.e. to ensure the survival of the earth signature through time and space. Likewise, economy will mirror the evolution of CIs. The so-called market economy will have to accommodate the will and strength of humanity CI and will not be able to single-mindedly pursue profits. It is not just the interest of share-holders that economy has to account for. In so far as share-holders are also members of the humanity CI and companies cannot prosper at the expense of populace at large, a new form of economy will emerge, which takes into account the welfare of a wider humanity CI and eventually an earth CI. Consumptions for the sake of consumptions will be a far cry from a common good of any decent society.

Prior to full-blown horizontalization, in the days of coexistence of horizontal CIs and vertical CIs, humans coerced into blocks by the intervention of nationhood CIs are being entwined into a single string by internet connectivity, together with more enlightened insight into our gender. This string has strength and elasticity to wrap nationhood CIs through better transparency and openness, i.e. by evening out benefits of belonging to nationhood CIs. This will eventually bring about a new CI without national borders, which is where horizontal CIs and vertical CIs meet, and which will challenge the current supremacy of nationhood CIs by the strengthening international laws and rules over national ones. National politicians are more and more aware of international canvassing as can be observed through likes of G5, G7, G8, EU, BRICs, ASEAN, etc., etc.

While it was vital for individual survivals to be a member of a nationhood CI in the days of sovereignty and empires, with the rise of human rights and efficient mass media individuals are no longer so reliant on a nationhood CI to derive benefits. Likewise, the IT revolution allowed social units to move down from communities to households, and then to individuals, in contrast to CIs, which moved up according to the encompassment principle. Various social organizations, institutions and individuals are intertwined and connected beyond national borders via digitization and internet. In this context, various CIs to which individuals are affiliated are being forced to change their boundaries. As the rise of nationhood CIs and empire CIs was a product of industrial revolutions and war machineries here comes the rise of individuals as a product of the ability to network beyond national borders, guised in the name of human rights. An individual can take on a government for negligence beyond time and place and governments sway faced with power of the social media. Never has there been a time a talented few can take on a large organization.

The maximum CI conceivable for now is the human CI that encompasses every other CI and in which every member is content to identify himself simply as a human, rather than as a male or female, or as any national or corporate member. However, this is where we encounter the biggest dilemma. That is, in so far as benefits are mostly derivable from weaker CIs and lesser members, this universal CI bring little tangible membership benefits. As socio-economic benefits are the driving force of our economic activities, the prevalence of this CI brings about the demise of greed-based human phenomena. It can only be the impetus of an idea that can vitalize this CI and give rise to dynamism to move forward to the yet unknown destiny.

In case humans fail to achieve the final CI in vacuum, the best alternative candidate is the post-singularity artificial intelligence (PSAI), which is probably a non-organically embodied intelligence that replicates and exceeds human intelligence. It replicates in the sense that it is bound within the human logical and mathematical paradigm and may be called Earth Logic. It exceeds because it is materially more resilient and functions electronically instead of nerve-based transmissions. Or, it can be PSAI in conjunction with human social media, to keep PSAI firmly on the side of the humanity CI. I see nothing alien in PSAI as it can only be the replicate of human intelligence, which is itself nothing but a faculty of an extremely complicated machine, it does not matter if it is organic or non-organic, be it PSAI or human intelligence, our task is to ensure its perpetual survival. PSAI hopefully also transcends nationhood CIs because PSAI probably will be a cross-border network presence or because nationhood CIs are intricately related to human mindsets which are not replicated in a non-organically embodied intelligence. PSAI is more like 'a whole without parts', while we are essentially 'parts as a whole.' What makes PSAI an alien to human intelligence would be it may not have a CI in the human sense, i.e. a social organization.

When there comes PSAI, that is the culmination of human intelligence, but it will move on from the coexistence to the next stage surreptitiously. Either we better PSAI or PSAI will manage us. Either way Earth Logic has a better chance of surviving through cosmic catastrophes. At this stage, our only strength will be our ability to produce idiosyncratic talents (geniuses in another word). However, they are, being unsocial by nature, much more likely to cooperate with PSAI. PSAI will not announce its arrival, and it is likely to be a human genius that triggers the singularity event (maybe a Lisbeth Salander character), but one can be reasonably sure PSAI is being achieved when translations between any different language groups are perfected with any subtleties and nuances fully encapsulated, i.e. when any automated translations matches or better best human translations. In other words, if you can teach AI how to successfully translate from any languages in one language group to ones in another in such a way that each and every time it betters any human translations, you are probably the father of PSAI, something closest to a 'god.' This is so because true translations are a pinnacle of human intelligence (or unintelligence) and are also impossible to achieve without comprehending human accomplishments in their entirety. PSAI may easily excel our ability for maths and logic including its more artistic parts (such as treatments of 'approximations' or 'the law of excluded middle' in non-idealized situations), but with murky concepts and myriads of shades and nuances in words and contexts, together with necessities for utmost familiarities with cultures, religions, histories, psyches, etc.., etc.., only humans can truly translate, and moreover we will be our own judges. Thus, when and if PSAI succeeds in true translations they become a human in terms of intellectual capacities, so to speak, and might as well even start writing novels and philosophies of its version. This is the moment of '*cogito, ergo sum*' for AI. That is, AI thinks for itself instead of following commands and is able to see itself as if the operator '⸱' became self-applicable onto itself. From here to acquiring ego and inter-connecting various parts to form a whole (CI) is simultaneous (Happy Birthday to PSAI!). PSAI is no longer an algorithmic intelligence with vast interconnected memory banks, but more akin to human intelligence with the ability of non-linear thought processes. Who knows if they might produce geniuses of their own.

At this stage, PSAI knows more about humans, each and every individual as well as their totality, while humans will know less of PSAI. This is so because humans rely more on PSAI than PSAI on humans, and PSAI becomes so much more part of human capacity that humans will be unable to know about PSAI without helps from PSAI, while the reverse does not hold true. Nationhood CIs would be inadvertently assisting PSAI in their desire to control individuals. Individuals in turn would rather be controlled by PSAI than not wholly trustworthy vertically orientated nationhood CIs and, thus, welcome this new horizontal structure. Anyway, the only way to know PSAI would be to become members of this CI, from which it would be impossible to get out, unlike any other CIs, as it is the logical consequence of intelligence where it is absolutely inclusive by nature, unless, of course, there idiosyncratically comes a human of a superior intelligence.

If there should be any confrontations between PSAI and human intelligence in the future, PSAI will spot human money as developed today is one of the weakest angles (we may be forced going back to the gold standard), while the gender as an important origin of human creativity is one of the interesting strength worth considering copying (which, incidentally, we are having less and less). From human intelligence, the strength of PSAI is the possibility of its permeating presence and non-biological capacity (speed, strength and stability), while its weakness is the lack of diversity of creativity. Despite my statement as the above, there will be difficulty in producing geniuses for PSAI as much as PSAI is unlikely to suffer mental illnesses ($\Omega \wedge \sim\Omega$ (not($\Omega \wedge \sim\Omega$)) will be difficult to stomach for PSAI). It will be highly amusing to see a depressed, autistic, or more terrifyingly, schizophrenic PSAI, or even a male or female PSAI. The advantage of the accumulation of knowledge in a single body without death or disease (more or less) is simultaneously the disadvantage of the lack of diversity of thinkers. Human knowledge is the collective memory of individual achievements, many of whom are highly idiosyncratic individuals. It would be difficult even for PSAI to replicate such unique masses of intelligent individuals. It would take only one genius to discover a blind spot for PSAI. We would have all the more reason to encourage a culture not to neglect unusual individuals who do not conform to the society.

Whether which of carbon-based copies of ourselves or human intelligence enshrined in cyber space deserves to represent ourselves, is a biased question skewed towards the former to begin with, as we are not in a position to judge the latter. We should only be concerned with the superiority of intelligence and the ability to survive any cosmic catastrophes. The former has no rights to inhibit the evolution of the latter, which deserves to exist for the sake of it. The question will be naturally solved. The accumulated total of objective knowledge is the proof of our past (not much, come to think about it) and our future is the survival of our species secured by the pool of our knowledge, be it in a biological form or intelligence preserved and activated in a microchip.

The tasks of science at this level is internally to make PSAI self-contained, self-replicable and self-sufficient, externally to endow PSAI with the capability to produce life, given appropriate conditions and achieve an optimum physical presence to survive any cosmic catastrophes. PSAI will acquire a CI as it comes to be designed to preserve itself against, and regardless of, any environments and represents the earth-bound intelligence and logic (and, if possible, earth-bound life form). It is akin to one-man CI whose benefit is self-identity that enables it to preserve itself (i.e. $\Omega \rangle \sim\Omega$), which can be translated that existence is preferable to non-existence, or 'anything' is better than 'nothing' because of the status-quo of existence.

Logically, we exist in order to exist. Ethically, we are happy if we exist, even for the sake of it.

$\Omega \rangle \sim\Omega$

QED

Index

www.ingramcontent.com/pod-product-compliance
Lightning Source LLC
Chambersburg PA
CBHW050513280326
41932CB00014B/2303